Praise

"Battista-Parsons' clever wording makes for vivid recreations of memories and food descriptions that make you hungry. Rich imagery teleports you from the kitchens of an Italian-American girl, to raw emotional explorations of beauty, love, and the difference between what we believe a woman should be and what a woman is. By the end of this memoir, I felt like I better knew the author, and better knew myself, as reading this reminded me of periods of my life as an Italian-American bambina. A must read to accompany bread and mozzarella Saturdays."

JUSTINE MANZANO, AUTHOR OF *NEVER SAY NEVER*

"If you're Italian-American, or even if you're not, be prepared for a sensual, passionate journey through the memoirs of a young woman's life. Filled with evocative images and details, Battista-Parsons' stories have viscerally broken through the snow. Her Italian bones and sensibilities are palpable throughout."

GLEAH POWERS, AUTHOR OF *MILLION DOLLAR RED*

About the Author

Elaina Battista-Parsons is a writer across genres. Elaina's poems, fiction, and essays have been published by *Backlash Press, Burnt Pine Magazine, The Spring City, 3Moon Magazine,* and *Read Furiously.* She also has an upcoming YA novel, *Black Licorice,* with Inked in Gray Press scheduled for fall 2022. Elaina loves ice cream, pop culture, and winter.

elainawrites.com

ITALIAN
BONES
IN THE
SNOW

a memoir in shorts

ELAINA BATTISTA-PARSONS

Italian Bones in the Snow
Copyright © 2022 Elaina Batista-Parsons

All rights reserved.
Print Edition
ISBN: 978-1-925965-82-7
Published by Vine Leaves Press 2022

Cover design by Jessica Bell
Cover images by
Interior design by Amie McCracken

 A catalogue record for this book is available from the National Library of Australia

For my brilliant daughters.
Listen softly and speak loudly when it counts.

Author's Note

A majority of the names have been changed to protect people's identities. My recollections are as close to the truth as I can remember. I write from a place rooted in love.

Contare I modi

To offer up what it's like to be a female, a daughter, a friend, a wife, and a witch of the winter requires you to give these pages a good hour, maybe two.

I am a cranky, goofy Italian-American girl who loves with all her heart. I am a happy fighter wielding her sword over the return of mom jeans, skinny jeans, and all things with suffocating buttons and zippers, really. That sword also likes to aim at people who don't know how to say thank you. That same sword won't hesitate to slash the egos of people who think they don't have more work to do on themselves. Newsflash: We all have big work to do. And we can't do it alone.

I am a musicologist who's hungry—for food and song and written words. Perhaps a beautiful roast beef sub with oil and vinegar from Jersey Mike's. I love *Golden Girls*, coal-fired pizza, and getting my neck adjusted. Twist, CRACK. Life.

Enjoy my Italian between the muscle
Nerves wrapped through the heart
Count the Ways:
Prose, Poetry, Dialogue, and
The threat of olive oil, garlic
If you stand too close to the stovetop,
it'll sting
But if you don't get close enough, you'll
never know the opulence

Uno

Infantile e Cosmica

Childish and Cosmic

Window Spray

Blue window spray is toxic if inhaled in large amounts. My guess might be that a child inhaling the fumes every Saturday afternoon for a few years straight might experience changes in the brain's chemicals, resulting in an intense over-thinker, who has the occasional panic attack during a full moon and stresses over the stakes in her novels. Or about whether she sucked up every braided dust ball under the couch with her fancy stick vacuum before her mom stops by. I sprayed a lot of blue window spray on paper towels as a kid. The blue liquid was pretty, and with just a few ice cubes, could be lemonade. The squeak on the glass was so damn satisfying at age ten. And if I had to clean, at least I got to use bright blue that smelled like electric July.

Besides blue window spray, our modest New Jersey house smelled like promise as I ate my own weight in black olives and cucumber spears with the zeal of an Olympian. My mom played Julio Iglesias's *Julio* as she prepared her incomparable dinners for company, and I stuffed my face with the aforementioned spears. Music, slicing, rich simmering, and the smell of blue window spray from earlier that afternoon warmed our 1978 Colonial style home.

Roast beef bits floating in brown gravy perfumed the house. Usually, if it was a Saturday, it meant we had company coming—often it was my mom's best friend, Lolly, a decisive and full-of-flair Jewish-American woman from Brooklyn. Sometimes it was our family friends, the Alts or Picones. Our life overflowed in friendship, and it was my job to prepare the living room for the friendship-food fest.

Earlier in the day before company, I'd dust the huge bookshelves in the living room. Then I had to wipe the interior portion of the windows with a blue spray that we all know the name of. The bookshelf I was in charge of was more of a display shelf—figurines from Greece, Italy, and my aunt's gift shop in Cranford, NJ. I remember a glass paperweight that had dried blue flowers melted and squished in the middle, and

ELAINA BATTISTA-PARSONS

I always wanted to crack it open. I wanted to pluck those flowers and crumble them in my fingers. I also remember a book—*Siddhartha*. My mom laid it on its side and used it as a base for a frame picture. I felt bad for it so I made it the star of the show. Italian moms are a special kind of fussy, so I'd get: "That's not right. Put it back the way I had it."

"But it—" I outstretched my arm and motioned to the better spot. The spot I chose.

"Put it back." She pointed to her spot with giant eyes eye-lined in black, then shadowed in soft purple.

"It's a nice bo—"

"Back." She planted her hands on her hips, dishtowel over shoulder.

I'd pop on Hall and Oates or Culture Club and remove every item from every shelf and table in the living room. I'd spray circles of lemon furniture spray (you know the one), and I'd wipe in satisfying circles using an older dishtowel. I shimmied to "Time Clock of the Heart" while I cleaned. Once every area was dust-free and dry, I'd place the items back in their designated spots. The glass paperweight with blue flowers inside begged me for a moment in the sunset. I'd move it over on the window side to catch the sun from the huge front window. My mom would return it to its original spot, but I always tried. I tried to pretend it was okay that my ideas were shot down without a consideration like, "Wow, it really does look better in the sunlight of 1985." Or, "Good thinking. I like it."

After lemons, came the blue spray. Blue spray on a paper towel, the sight of a god-close cleanliness. Ammonia parfait. Chemical bliss. Circles and circles. More spray. Vitality so blue and toxic. I couldn't screw up circles and paper towels. Except I could.

"Not like this, like that. Don't you know by now?" She grabbed the tools out of my grip.

"But—"

"Like this." She moved as if she was being graded, judged, then categorized.

As the sun would begin to set, the house simmered in a closer-to-complete brown gravy and now, bits of onion. Or maybe the house sizzled in tomato sauce divinity. Depended. All I knew was that company was on their way, and the raw fennel and cucumber was mine for the taking. Behind the good food, and

secretly the star of the show, was the blue liquid
that graced those glass windows and left no streaks.
Because my mom checked my work. Repeatedly. In
circles that squeaked and sang of blue sunshine in a
bottle that could kill you if consumed because what
appears beautiful hides the blisters on a kid's spirit.

The 1980s sang of pinks, greens, blues
Volume on one thousand
Tasting like bubblegum
At one glance,
One slushy gulp.
One six-inch bangs cluster

Growing up in this
Cavalcade of pop music
Candy
Made you
Expect

Growing up with company over—
Cake and Coffee.
It sets you up to wonder where the laughter is
Every Saturday, Sunday
Your stirred-up childhood

Dims this adulthood
Then again
We eat real lettuce now
And we don't smell like our
Parents' cigarettes

ELAINA BATTISTA-PARSONS

First Time Here?

I bet I lived on East 68th Street in New York City in my past life—an Ethel Mertz in my A-line orchid cocktail dress, fussing with my face powder and yapping with Lucy about where we're going for our Friday out with the fellows. Will we see a show after our veal chop and mashed potato dinner in the city? Was I the cooperative best friend ready for my tenacious friend's next adventure across the carpets of Bloomingdale's?

Maybe this way of thinking could be a disrespect to those who really are reincarnated? There are people out there who can't shake it because the sensations and flashes of their first life keep them up at night and cause palpable fear. It's much more complex than feeling déjà vu or having a wild imagination about where you might have lived once. It's not impossible that my feelings are legit, but likely it's my writer's imagination and a wish to have that memory of my soul being recycled. A wish to know that I might have cared that my husband sat with his newspaper and ate eggs and drank black coffee before he caught a cab to the Tropicana to sing "Babalú."

An old soul attaches to a newly born soul. That's the crux of reincarnation, causing the new soul to relive things and recall moments from the old life, sending the new person into a frenzy at night, or amidst a storm, or in the middle of blood being drawn. I suppose the memories can flood in at any given time. I assume it's never convenient and not always pleasant. Particularly if the new soul is remembering how the past life died. It can't be easy to experience these flashbacks. I empathize with those who have no choice in the matter. I empathize with that kind of soul drain. It's probably exhausting.

Is being reincarnated the difference between loving the preparation of a lunch dish midday while other women hate every second of it? Or have I watched and reveled in too many *I Love Lucy* episodes, and they've made me treasure simplicities of the home, particularly season six in Connecticut? Or do the memories of my grandmothers and their fabulousness reign too strong for me so that I cannot tell the difference? Me, a former 1940s housewife a la Ethel Mertz, and the other kitchen-despising women, brand new souls who never experienced the comfort of a clean kitchen? Prepping a ham and cheese on rye with a pickle makes me feel good. Memory of a past life, or a basic personality trait? This doesn't mean I enjoy all aspect of housekeeping. In fact, it's the only one I enjoy. Cleaning toilets can suck it.

To be honest, my dreams at night never include being a 1940s housewife. Instead, my dream state slaps a highly uncomfortable 1990s style dress on my body, a million boxes and things strewn about my dream's setting (usually a hotel). Items must be packed up so that I can catch my flight to France. The flight I never make. I have yet to see Paris in my dreams. Does this mean I was a French hoarder in my past life? I'm the opposite in my current life, so is it that I learned from the catastrophe of clutter in my first life and became an Italian purger? Or maybe it's because I've moved/relocated close to thirteen times in my actual life.

Moments seem to be significant in feeling how old our souls are if reincarnation does exist. Why did you feel that chill up your spine when your friend mentioned the word *chartreuse*? Did the photograph of the antique store in downtown Asbury Park, NJ bring a brassy scent through your nostrils as if you smelled it many times before? Why are certain names of people in the forefront of our brains—names that have no meaning in our current existence? Then of course, dreams.

Exploring these ideas is worth something to me. To science. To our humanity. Similar to understanding the history of politics and disease, understanding humanity at this level could reveal answers about ourselves. Answers might exist in places we never thought possible. Places we go to when we sleep, dream, or meditate on a bench by the ocean. I realize many of you are rolling your eyes and dismissing this kind of thinking, and that's okay. It might mean you're new here. Or you are dead set on the science you can see clearly. Your next body might acknowledge your current life. Ooh! Maybe you'll be a hummingbird next and recognize the kitchen window by the sink where you once rinsed blueberries. Or a high school science teacher in Idaho, and when your student mentions their parents were born in New York, you'll know you've been on this earth once before. My therapist happens to believe that everyone was once someone else. I disagree. I think some of us are brand new.

ELAINA BATTISTA-PARSONS

When I was about nine or ten years old I'd take summertime naps in my parents' bedroom on occasion. I grew up on the Jersey Shore. Theirs was the only room in the house with an air conditioning unit. It was usually a day where I was up with the robins, running in circles around the neighborhood with friends, on my bike, gathering twigs, grass, and tick-infested weeds. Sometimes if my mom was off from work, it would be a beach morning—a seven a.m. until four p.m. kind of day. After the long beach day, I was ready for a quick afternoon nap to the sound of my neighbor's lawnmower. My body was sun and sea weary. And I'd have the same dream every time: I had to hold up clay boulders with toothpicks. Or maybe they were rocks. And my body was invisible in the dream. I was simply a force. The same dream, only in late afternoons, and only in the summer. For about two years. I still remember it. Was that part of a past life memory? Maybe.

This next part, regarding Reiki, is going to lose those with lofty religious guilt sitting on their chest. Which is interesting to me because I don't think religion should have any say or role in the energies around us. The messages from loved ones. I am by no means a true Catholic anymore. The Catholic Church as an institution gives me the same feels as cleaning those toilets. If you forget, skim backwards in this section. You'll see it. They can keep their antiquated thinking, their politics, and their disillusionment. You can keep your old ways that damage peoples' hearts, Mr. Catholic Church. Until you recognize gay marriage as real marriage, we cannot be friends, and I am not stuttering. Until you recognize that women can also be the "head of the household" you will have no part in my life. The only part of the religion that interests me is the rosary because it's about the Mother, and she's the part I honor. Her watch. Her guidance. Her matriarchy. She's the head of the household.

I circle back. Never once in my practice of Reiki have I felt like I was betraying anyone or anything high above in the clouds. In fact, quite the opposite. In some ways, energy practice is a nod to our spirituality. Usui Ryoho's style of Reiki addresses the whole person on the physical, emotional, mental and spiritual levels. It's the practice of using the palm of a practitioner's hands on areas of the recipient's body that require unblocking. It's very similar to the way acupuncture needles work.

I found Reiki out of pure luck when I threw my lower back out in my early thirties. My friend Stephanie asked me to seat myself in child's pose. She gently placed her hands on my lower back and I felt waves from her fingertips. The next day, I was upright. I asked her what she did. "Reiki," she said.

It's opened doors for me, using my three favorite examples. Believe if you like. I have no reason to lie. I could tell you dozens of more instances, but this is not a book about Reiki. The other thing I need to make clear is that I am not a healer. No one is. The energy in our own bodies is the healer. Humans are the conduit. Stop putting healer on your profile description. We all have it in us to do this kind of work, so it's a choice. Not a special gift. Enjoy the three of many anecdotes from my life. Names are changed to protect friends.

One: I was ten months pregnant and my spiritual radar was highly active. I was upstairs getting ready for a holiday party at our cousin's house on the lagoon, nearby. As I put the emerald green sweater over my head, then my round belly, I saw a flash behind my eyelids: "Jane. ER."

"Honey. Jane is in the ER," I said to my husband as I applied my lipstick in the kitchen, and we gave our babysitter instructions.

"What?" he said, buttoning up his sleeves, then folding them up.

"I don't know," I said, dabbing the last of my brick red.

"Whatever you say." He rubbed my belly, then kissed our baby girl in utero.

We arrive at the party, crack open our drinks and begin picking at the appetizer platters. My husband asks his cousin where Jane was.

"Oh. She's in the ER. Her daughter hurt her ankle."

I'm pretty sure he spit his beer across the room.

Two: Imposter Syndrome sets in for artists often. Usually right before a breakthrough on a project, or before a piece of news that gets their ass in gear again. So I laid on my bed, in hormonal-driven tears crying hard and with attention to my dear lost friend, Bob, who had died a few years prior at the young age of forty. "Bob. Tell me what to do. Should I stop writing and give up? Give me a sign that you can hear me. PLEASE."

The next morning I called my eye doctor who I see once a year for my old eyes. My 20/20 eyes, surprisingly still, but old, nonetheless. The front desk put me on hold. Cue the waiting instrumentals. "Hi. Can I help you?"

"Yes I need to make a yearly appointment."

"Okay. And you said your birthdate is 12/18?"

"No. I didn't say anything. We didn't speak yet. But can I ask you why you said that date?"

"I have no idea why."

"Well, that's the birthday of my friend who died and I asked him for a sign."

"OH MY GOD I believe in this stuff, and I have always wanted to give someone a message."

"Well, you just did. Thank you."

Three: My dear friend from college required absentee Reiki in 2021. She was in extreme medical danger from COVID-19. Absentee Reiki is done with an intricate string of Japanese symbols and training. I can work on the recipient from afar. I worked on her. I saw the name CARL behind my eyes in a swirl of smoky black letters. I told her sister what I saw.

Her sister revealed that her ICU nurse is Carlo. How could I know this? I didn't. I saw the name behind my eyes during the Reiki symbolism practice.

I share these few instances for one reason—to show you that energy is real. There is no way these examples were coincidental, particularly because I have about twenty more.

This here physical life on Earth is only part of our journey. However, I do think it's likely as touchable and delicious as it'll get. I think *on* Earth is where the goods are—shrimp cocktail, live music, nerve endings. Eat that ice cream, and say I love you. The other side may not be as concrete. Or maybe it's *more* textural? I guess one day we will all know.

It's important I add this last note about my children's CCD (religious education) experience. In addition to the Virgin Mary, the other part of Catholicism that interests me is the bonding that happened with loved ones. Growing up with two widowed Italian grandmothers who loved church on Sundays, my brother and I would often sit with them. I couldn't tell you a word that was uttered by the priest, but what I do remember is their hands holding ours. Their soft hands, the look of solace on their faces, and the closeness we felt to them. I remember the smell of sage burning. Everything but the religion became my religion in that moment. Yola and Josephine outlived their husbands by decades and made good lives for themselves, full of family and modest living. My church was my grandmothers. Their veiny hands and the love in their eyes. The smell of their lipstick. I experienced a boatload of cognitive dissonance about raising my girls in any one religion. We pray together at bedtime, but quite universally, with no doctrine or bible attached to our words. I never use the masculine as a guiding force. I didn't even buy it as a kid.

Enter CCD instruction: I found myself reteaching and course-correcting with my daughters constantly: "The man is not always the head of the household. Yes, two women or two men can get married and be recognized as a real marriage. Divorce is okay."

I cannot have my girls thinking in patriarchal terms. And I certainly cannot have them thinking that marriage is only designed for two cisgender heterosexuals. My husband and I do the work there too. I pulled them out of CCD recently when it finally hit me that I was being hypocritical to think that it was just "tradition." My church died when my grandmothers died. Now we visit the Mary statue in outdoor spaces whenever we can. We may even sit in our upstairs loft and pray to her statue. Light a candle for those in need. It's so complex, our relationships to our religious roots. All I care about is that they know there's a higher power. That's it. Whether it's the trees in our yard, a bird, Buddha, an idea of sky and air, anything. If they want to convert to Judaism, that works too. If they want to explore Hinduism, awesome. My husband has a great view of religion: don't be an asshole. I concur.

Gumballs

Growing up, my dad had a love for gumball machines, and we noticed. My brother and I knew it stemmed from his own childhood. A sort of carried on tradition. He had a good childhood in Newark, with a caring older sister, a nurturing mom, and a dad who worked as many jobs possible in order to pay the bills. They lived close to family and everyone was always together. All of the stores downtown had vending machines, and the notion of popping in a penny then pulling a lever or a knob fascinated my dad to no end. It was the mechanics that tickled him, and then of course, the prize at the end. His childhood was all about "penny prizes," and so by having these machines in the house as an adult, he could relive that joy.

Most of the time, the gumball machines we had in my childhood home on Mulberry Place were empty, like he couldn't decide between aesthetic or function. Not until I had my own children did the gumballs in Poppy's home flow with no boundaries. He is partial to the square Chiclets, and my girls like to pop the pennies, pull the lever to the side and wait for their three or four pieces to spit out the chute.

I want to form thin marker geometry when I see you
I imagine you living
A super tiny heart
Pumping super tiny sugar blood

Spherical
orbital perfection
bright markers, feverish
papaya-juice
lemon-pop
mint-perfume
Sirens singing hymnals into my
tongue, teeth, big bursts of pink, yellow, and green
your heart's explosion
glorious

Fairground carousel bliss
as if I'm seven years old

ELAINA BATTISTA-PARSONS

biting in
crushed berries and diamond mangoes
granules of bliss
sweet, sour
gumballs
explode and sway me into believing anything

Cemetery

My childhood bedroom on Mulberry Place faced a cemetery. It sat behind the neighbors' house across the street from us, so the view was crisp and wide. I recognized from a very young age, that this view was a gift. It comforted me. Those rows and expressions of headstones in silence among floral tapestries, mature trees, all crafted in such peaceful flow. Most man-made presentations bored me, but not this one because, though the stones were fabricated, the peace was not.

The cemetery lay only yards behind the woods that cradled our neighborhood treehouse, waiting for us to feel humbled by its manor-like presence. Gorgeous and dead. Thistled mortality. Elegant ghouls partner in the night for a waltz, reminding the neighborhood below to listen to the moon as she delegates. Manages.

October, November, the rows of headstones made me want to revel in the season so deeply. Pockets full of holly and juniper berries fell from the trees that lined the space. Poisonous walnuts stunk up parts of the ground. An exercise in enchantment. But also in sweaty, greasy skin depression as a kid. That scorching sun on my face all day, then a washing of sadness over me. I couldn't share or identify depression out loud in words back then. So instead, I'd get a headache and wonder about it. I was overwhelmed with ideas of death and art and nature, all the time.

Our older Russian neighbor named Nora Pavloff had the best view of the cemetery. The closest. Nora was tall and thin with the tidiest white hair and long, unpainted fingernails. She always wore scratchy-looking polyester pants, even in summer. Her dog, Tiger, was the sweetest girl in the world. Nora would serve the neighborhood kids cookies and soda, when all we really wanted was to sneak a peek from her second floor—stones, flowers, graves, mature trees guarding all of it. French vanilla dirt roads. Powdery dust trails from cars feeling fresh loss. Weeping. I ate the cookies but swallowed my wishes. I didn't dare to ask about staring at death.

ELAINA BATTISTA-PARSONS

God, how I wanted to get a close-up, bird's eye view of the names on the headstones from her upstairs window.

My cemetery sang both arias and rock ballads, depending on the time of year. And it loved the dead of February: cleaning, peace-extending, with a pop of ruby. I buried my sad thoughts in the soil. That dirt was more understanding of my ways than anything with spring sprouts, green, or bright yellow. Cold earth knew me better.

Dead people
under
stones that taste like fairytales
friendships I never had
headaches for days

DEB

It originates from the word debutante. I had no idea about this as a kid and found out only more recently. Did you know Deb stores were established in 1932 during the Great Depression? What I do know is DEB clothing store carpets looked like they should've smelled like strawberry lip gloss, not stale hot pretzel and thick dust. I remember the dressing rooms being wide (at least in our mall down here), and the speakers blowing up "I Think We're Alone Now" by Tiffany—my anxious little twelve-year-old heart, all jittery. My body tingly in wrong, but *such* right ways. I'd always find a purple shirt or bright green skirt on the clearance rack, complementing my budget, while my high-banged bff would have a forearm full of fabric. Pounds of options, but no matter. I was happy to be out shopping. I remember the white lights encased in plastic, framing the dressing room doors and the new display of outfits on platforms. 1980s clothes stores chose pageantry, didn't they?

The mall itself glowed in Hot Sam saltiness and cheap blue eyeshadowed teenagers. Painted in denim. God, I miss the '80s glamour and spectacle sometimes. I could really go for a tray of pretzel sticks and fake melted cheese. Wash it down with a nice thick Orange Julius.

Newark in my Mouth

Prosperity:
the name of my inner
hairy-armed kid's texture memory
scarved in wool
Gram in a magenta silk scarf
my boots tight and cranky
that wool scarf making me nuts
itchy, a sensory nightmare
Thankfully the rest of the memory overflows with love

"Prosperity," Gram would say
as cookie crumbs flew from her wrinkled lips
She had to finish her coffee before we bundled up

The deli called Prosperity Market—
canned pepper castles

across metal shelves.
Italian grocer flattens
fresh tenderloins
cheese in water waiting to be chosen by
Elsie,
Concetta, or
Max

Prosperity dripping from my eyelids
down my chin
my tears
Now my dreams of her
Gram's arm in mine

On the way to Prosperity

ELAINA BATTISTA-PARSONS

Lunar Chunk

I long to speak to a piece of the moon
perhaps a small section can
descend the gossamer ladder
onto my stacked milkcrates
engineered
in the night of my eight-year-old heart
made of crayon dust

I step on a pile of brown and red oak leaves, now at 44
I ask this lunar chunk
What comes next?
How does breath win?
How do we walk around anymore
among the sun-dried matter
The land of the
"I'm going to do what I want anyway?"

What about everyone else?
What about those who need us too?

What happened to caring for the greater good?

ELAINA BATTISTA-PARSONS

Goblins and Greens

I had that uncle in NYC that chose cerebral and sophisticated gifts for my brother and me when we were kids. Hardcover books from MOMA, wooden puzzles, and maps to places unknown, probably made by a cartographer who also played oboe for the philharmonic. What teen *doesn't* want a miniature replica of a baritone horn in a case?

The one thing he always gave us which we truly loved were the Chinese yo-yos on a stick. He was the same uncle who lived in the Upper West side apartment adorned in cats at every corner (live ones) and a long-hair-braided wife who hung old Victorian style boots and hats on the walls. Quintessential brownstone in a pre-gentrified NYC. I think they were costume boots from The Metropolitan Operas in which she was a chorus member, and others simply collectors' items probably snagged from antique stores around the country. I loved visiting him in the city when I was a kid, probably eight or nine years old to begin.

When you entered his apartment, a very narrow hallway led to his tiny kitchen, then larger den/dining that led to the back "yard." The entrance hallway was one giant bookshelf wall full of odd objects that balanced on one leg and stacks of large photography books. The lighting was dim, the way I prefer my life. I can't stand bright lighting and never could. There was a lot of dark wood in that apartment. Operatic itself. And if you turned left instead of right upon entering, there was a very small sleeping space that overlooked the Hudson River and included a spiral staircase that led to the master bedroom. Nothing like our homes in suburban NJ. His wife had a lot of purple everywhere: quilts, shawls, and bathtub rugs. The floors all black and white tiles, some hexagonal and others round.

And then the book. The book that I believe has a lot to do with my love for literature and all it is capable of: magic, impact, drama, freedom: *The Rainbow Goblins* by Ul de Rico. If you have not seen or read it, it's a book originally written in German but translated to English. The goblins' faces are demonic. The kind that children love to be terrified by, but also, comforted by. The actual word goblin tickled me. If you google it, you'll see the words grotesque spirit. Now that's a phrase worth storing in your brain for later.

The Rainbow Goblins is a remarkable book with striking illustrations and a premise about the rainbow's purpose. More or less, a legend. I remember learning what the word treachery meant, as the back cover read: a classic tale of treachery and virtue. It was like no other picture book we owned back in the New Jersey suburbs. It felt darker, but also more vulnerable. Which is why I think it is so important to expose children to all kinds of art from a very young age. If you can't afford to travel, then buy or borrow all kinds of books by writers from cultures other than your own. My brother and I chose our favorite colors from the crew of goblins who were tangled up in the lasso when they were trying to steal the rainbow. It became a thing.

Our birthday and Christmas gifts reflected these color choices: flashlights, pens, and all of the other unique NYC uncle type gifts. I forgot about the goblin book until my thirties when I had my own children and began reading them everything wonderful and unique. I bought a new copy and tried to relive the mystique with my children, and though they kind of liked it, it didn't have the same impact. Being read to in that dimly lit brownstone of a space, with red and black leather couches and creepy boots on the wall—that's what was missing for my kids. Oh, and the cats pouncing from one shelf to the next with every page turn. I remember their names: Agamemnon (Aggie), Antigone (Tiggy), and Pete.

After *The Rainbow Goblins* was read to us repeatedly anytime we visited my uncle, my brother and I became glued to the idea of his color being yellow and mine, green. We liked the goblins of those colors too. The yellow goblin was the leader. The green one, merely commenting on the creamy texture of the rainbow's colors. Thinking about this color designation at a young age gave me this idea of separating our life into a paint swatch of a chosen color family, almost the way artists like Picasso had the Blue Period, etc. I barely know anything about his art, but I know about my greens.

Kindergarten Green

I always loved grabbing color swatches from wallpaper stores in the 1980s when they were a thing, and now from Lowes and Home Depot. I'd cut them up then shuffle them as if they were tarot cards, having no idea what a tarot card was. The spreads just felt right. I utilized those swatches when I taught third grade. I asked my students to rename them when we were studying descriptive language. How many names for pale pink can we come up with? Many, it turns out. It recently occurred to me that maybe those colors are secretly portals to another place and time. Like Kindergarten, for one. In the early 1980s Kindergarten consisted of a lot of coloring "dittos" using designated colors for designated objects: purple grapes, orange oranges, yellow suns, green trees.

Green. I am very drawn to its flavor and its presence. I want to enter that true green portal for a moment. Let's name it first. Kindergarten Green feels like a perfect name, actually.

I imagine the entrance into the paint swatch portal to resemble that smooth texture of the swatch. You'd simply close your eyes, run your hand over the color, and sink into its veneer, like a cookie cutter into dough.

Kindergarten Green surrounds you, and you slide into it, like landing in a May afternoon full of buzzing and seedlings. Like a wish for crisp snap peas or the perfect leaf from a Walnut tree contrasted against a cherry tomato or those red bubblegum balls that shine more than they should.

Once you're in the Kindergarten Green door
hear the sounds:
the loose wheels of the milk wagon
up and down the school hallways
toward the cafeteria
the crackly narration of the Scholastic stories
on cassette told by a narrator
that sounds like a grandma you love
she has that affect that can't be faked
The crayons in the small plastic box when shaken

My heart's Ga-Bump as we sing songs
with bells in Music Class
The squeak of smelly markers in Art Class
my favorite being lime

Hunter Green

Hunter Green was the color of my homecoming dress my sophomore year in high school. It had a tuxedo front, sleeveless, and had a dropped V-neck. My mom definitely wasn't against me wearing something figure-flattering, having gone to New York fashion school. She made certain my dresses were a combination of appropriate and form-fitting. And always fashion-forward. Hunter Green was very 1990s, but the style was timeless. That dress made her debut in 1992. The thing I remember most was shaving a chunk of my ankle hours before my high school boyfriend arrived for photos with two other couples. I had to wear a huge square band aid (more like gauze pad) on my right ankle all night under my pantyhose. Yes, we all wore pantyhose during colder months with our dresses. Nobody wants to see a bloody ankle ooze through pantyhose at homecoming.

Hunter Green was the second green chapter of my life. Jump into that swatch, headfirst, with the soundtrack of "Salvation!" by The Cranberries, then half of Pearl Jam's "State of Love and Trust." You're a little nauseated from that portal's pull, but you arrive safely in the apartment you owned with your first husband. Your napkins are Hunter Green, his Jeep the same color. The sounds are extremely different from Kindergarten Green, now at twenty-four years old.

You hear wind
You hear tears
You hear fighting
You hear a lot of music
and it's solid music, so at least there's that
I must give thanks to that Hunter Green Jeep
that took me through the Ozarks
Blue Ridge, off road
up and down mountains
hair in knots
The Church's classics, Queens of the Stone Age, Incubus
and a lot more Cranberries, post '90s
Tori Amos pokes her head in too
those twinkly piano keys shake you silly

You smell Sunday sauce
in that cat-hair-dusty apartment
You see stressed foreheads
You see guitars
You smell meatballs simmering
You hear church bells and cats scratching at pillows
You trip over long dress trains and wipe
your snot with its giant bell sleeves.
half-priced Sushi Sundays
with friends freshly married too

Then you taste marital disaster, divorce, screams
but it's leading you somewhere else
so hang on tight
for the next green of your swatch
Stay hydrated

New England Green

This paint square is the most sit-down-with-a-cup-and-tea-and-breathe green. Which was close to impossible and not even a microscopic thought in my head before age thirty-two. This green represents the time when that steaming mug feels like home. Think Sage Green, but I like the comparison to New England where there are mountains, country roads, covered bridges, and random maple syrup markets waiting for your vulnerable heart to open up.

Jumping into this portal, you'll see hiking trails, lush gardens, Christmas tree farms, landscapes, rocking chairs, and a lot of dusty bookshelves surrounding the perfect chair and end table. Perhaps in Woodstock, Vermont, or a café in Princeton, New Jersey? This green sounds like post-2000 Tori Amos, Thin Lizzy, and acoustic versions of all your favorite songs. Some Colin Hay, live and folksy, Ani DiFranco tangled in the creamy green sage paint. Toss in a little Florence + the Machine and Fleetwood Mac.

You're here in the Sage Green swatch and it smells like chamomile and mint. You're able to let someone love you for real. You can exhale a little bit. You know a bit more about people and life, and you're able to say no to things that make your insides clench and your scalp itch. Even if you once said yes, you know better now that it's okay to change your mind and grow. Sage Green is edging toward mid-life, which means you no longer have to wear jeans that button or zipper up. Elastic waistbands are fine because no one will ever know. And because you have too many things to accomplish in a day—you need movement. Leverage. In the Sage Green portal lives arugula-topped pizza and vodka with seltzer. On a Tuesday while sitting in a recliner and reading a book. Your kids can keep themselves busy. But don't get too comfortable because, in the Sage Green world, you get acid reflux more easily and you can pull a back muscle from sneezing. No matter how great of shape you're in.

Sage Green brings real love. Laugh until you burst kind of love. Language of laundry love. He's always there for you, love.

The thing I enjoy about the paint swatch portals is that they can overlap at any time. When we write or create or socialize, the greens choose themselves, make themselves present, and guide us. When we dream, shout, cry, or protest, they smudge and mix. It's never so clean and tidy, unless it is.

Having children affects the swatch color you live in. Maybe you're more of a blue or gray. Sometimes I like to dive into the deep dark purples. Green seems to be the easiest for me to write about right now for some reason I can't explain. Next time you're in a paint or home store, grab a few. Keep them nearby. Jump.

Due

Guardami, Sono Carina

Look at me, I'm Pretty

Madonna Mia

Two people in my family have encountered Madonna. My uncle had a full conversation with her in a gas station, at which she inquired about the old-school Playboy bunny tattoo on his shoulder. She told her driver to approach my uncle to see if he minded a chat with her. He treated her like anyone else. Which is why she kept talking, and why I'll never meet her. The planets say, HELL NO to me but my uncle was different because he was unfazed. Impressive, if you ask me. The most interesting part of this encounter for me is the universe's role. Madonna and my uncle both grew up without one of their parents—she, her mother, and my uncle, his father. Plus, their birthdays are fourteen days apart. My uncle probably recalls this experience as a cool thing that happened one summer day. Meanwhile,

I can't let it go. I've been studying her since eighth grade. Admittedly, my studies sort of slowed down in the past ten years, but still. He had an encounter with one of the greatest pop icons to ever live, and he never flinched. We could all learn from that.

The other Madonna encounter was with my aunt who sang with the Metropolitan Opera and happened to be in the waiting room of their mutual vocal doctor. I guess that would be an otolaryngologist. I don't believe they exchanged words, only a smile or nod. I figure I have to be the third person to meet her? Things come in threes, but I know deep down it's never going to happen. The universe would rather implode. I'd be frozen. Pun intended. My heart would be open, but my mouth would unravel scratchy yarn, and my words would cut holes in her eyeballs from their sharp awkwardness. Her eyebrows would scrunch: *Whoa. Are you okay? A glass of water perhaps?*

Only I notice her muscular hamstrings when she bends over the bleachers in *A League of Their Own,* getting a glimpse of Madonna-trademark strength, forgetting about All-the-Way Mae. Only I connect how we both have those same strong legs. In an interview, she once commented that her favorite features included her hands and her back. No mention of her legs. If you watch the video for "Vogue," you will see her twisting and showcasing her back and hands to boast their magnetism. I still say her legs give her the most agency. When you think of Madonna, you know exactly what I am talking about. Thighs of something more than steel. Superior materials, girls.

I am her. She is me. One of my moons. My artistic alphabet. Eighth grade was when my guts began falling out over Madonna and I imagined that she and I were two Italian-American artists with not enough time on Earth to say it all. Only you *know* her, and likely will only know me for this book and maybe a few others. Which is more than I could ask for, really. I've had many dreams where she sits and tells me things, and usually it's "Just do it. Try." So I do. Ridiculous obsession? Maybe. My favorite Madonna songs: too many to count, but I'll name just two: "Skin" and "Angel." Her activism and generosity in her personal life means more to me than any of her songs.

I attempt to reinvent
show the world that female is platinum
roots so strong, you die trying to break us

strong legs, strong eyes, endless hunger
with a pinch of garlic.
Lady Madonna
not the one with child
blue dress. white dress. no dress.

But it means something
to reinvent our spirits
for the next phase
the next push toward immortality

ELAINA BATTISTA-PARSONS

Wintered Earth

I woke up to white. White lawns. White dog blossom trees. Icicled gutters. The snow was falling sideways and the flakes were larger than my bitten thumb nails. Visibility totally compromised. It fell in sync with the loss of everything I had shed—virginity and the pristine high school reputation that was saturated in my clothes in my closet. I still had a few extra pounds on my thighs, but those could wait until I returned to dorm life in about two weeks.

Right now, the snowstorm beckons me like it did the girl in that William Steig book, *Brave Irene*. She had a pink gown. I had an ache. I had to see my boyfriend before he left for six months of army boot camp. My almost nineteen-year-old heart belonged to him and he was leaving for six whole months. That was eternity in teenage years. Leaving me to finish semester two at my private university an hour from our sea-salty hometown. And like Brave Irene, minus the ball gown for the duchess, I had to walk six miles in this sideways, burning blender of snow and ice. It would be my pleasure, despite my mom cursing me (not at me) as I really took those steps down the silent snow-covered street of my neighborhood. I was born in a snowstorm. It was home to me somewhere deep in my soul's software.

My cheeks sparkled in January, like the tree silhouettes against the sky. We tiptoed and breathed the same way. Like an oboe and a flute written by Tchaikovsky. My hair had grown to mid-shoulder length, now perfectly straight until the wet snowflakes got their hands on my Italian hive. I chose a hat with a white pom-pom because how cute and sweet against the heavy, bulky snow pants needed for today. He'd say, "Your cheeks." Then he'd kiss them with the speed of our Earth's orbit. This storm was merciless and the sensation of being soaked to the bone when you have miles left was harsh. The wind yelling—it was like a bass being slapped with blistered hands. Painful thrums of the Flea-type.

A mile in, I felt the abandonment. The town was asleep, and an air of deep winter began a melody to which I'd never be able to locate the harmony. Roads were closed, sidewalks layered in white cake. So thick and slippery, and I stood in the middle of major highways because no cars were in sight. Surreal. Both beautiful and terrifying. Alone in streets of a town that were normally jammed up and full of friction. The only sound was the wind pulling the snow, making my walk a slog. I wanted to feel his pink lips on mine before he left. His tongue on my teeth. His smell on my neck one more time before late spring when he'd return home to our large suburban town with four distinct sections and personalities. Which was now encased in cold, thick snow. Brave like Irene.

By mile four I was wiped. And not in the good way like the night before this whitewashed scene of January 1996. Last night I was swimming in sweat—his and mine. A pen in the snow stuck out like a hand reaching up to me, asking to be used in love letters, I supposed. But in a storm where paper would melt and crumble, I shoved the blue pen into my thick, poofy vest pocket. My hands were frozen despite my wool gloves. I thought of Irene again and winced. The air was blade-like, and the snow relentless. Two more miles before I'd see his stubbled face. The recruiter surely wouldn't beat me to his house. It was only 8:45 in the morning.

Unlike other snowstorms, no children were playing outside anywhere. Either they were devouring their pancake stacks or their moms were not letting them go into this funnel. I entered the part of town where the main street shops stood deserted, and I couldn't help but notice the storybook charm of the old downtown. Antique storefronts, banks, and a closed coffee shop. If only I could feel my toes. My boots were supposed to be insulated. Perhaps a mileage limit should be indicated on these items: not good for long, arduous walks to see your lover in a snowstorm. You know, the boyfriend whose mouth was like strawberries. The boyfriend you lost your virginity to the night before.

With numb hands and toes I closed my eyes, squatted in the middle of what would be main street traffic if it were spring, and thought about why I was here in the first place. Why, like Brave Irene, had I decided to trek miles on this frigid winter day. She had her mom's handsewn pink ballgown. I had nothing to deliver but my face on his. His blue eyes. His blond eyelashes and how he saved me from myself. From becoming what everyone expected of senior class president. No one really had any expectations of me, except me, but the narrative refused to cease in the depths of my veins. He showed me other things

ELAINA BATTISTA-PARSONS

that made life worth living, rather than constant planning and achieving. A story as old as leather or Sunday meatballs. Bad boy, but brilliant boy gives all-around ambitious pretty girl the gift of truth and sunshine. His delicious, warm sex.

I stood up and walked forward. Inches away, a red Jeep Cherokee pulled up beside me, coming from up a narrow side street. "Hop in. It's freezing out here," said a kind man with gray hair and a ski jacket. He tilted his head and scratched his cheek and somehow that indicated to me he was friend, not foe.

"I don't know you," I said, and continued walking as the Jeep rolled alongside me. My pace was firm, but my toes were ice cubes at this point.

"That is true. We are driving around picking up medical professionals who need a ride to the hospital. You clearly are on a mission to get somewhere important." He smiled and I could tell it was the truth. I also noticed the woman in her pom-pom hat next to him which I hadn't noticed initially. I hopped in.

The rest of the trip warmed my limbs, yet caused my heart to shiver, shrouded in a sad type of anticipation. Hall and Oates on the local station.

Would I beat the army recruiter to his house? Would he be as sad to say goodbye as I was to him? I wasn't his first, but he swore he loved me. He swore we were amazing together and that we'd survive a few months apart. He told me to lean on Bob, my dorm friend and resident rockstar with the cigarettes and guitar.

I did beat the recruiter, but only by five minutes. My boyfriend was organizing his duffle bag and startled by my devotion to get there in the blizzard. We exchanged a silent goodbye that contradicted the entire six months leading up to it. The ache to be near him all the time. The passion of our first kiss on the beach last May. His hand on my cheek was cold like the outside, but his hug felt like an oven. The guitar I gave him for Christmas lay out of its case on his bed. He was messing around with it while he waited to be picked up. I could tell he was protecting his heart by not being overly emotional.

"Don't cry. I love you," he said and then giggled the way he giggled. All dirty blond and tasty. "I'll see you in a few months. It's okay." He moved a curl from my eyebrows and sniffed it in. Exhaling deeply.

"Be careful. Please write to me," I said, swallowing my sob. "Here." I gave him the pen. Might as well have been my heart too.

"I will. All the time." The giggle was lost, replaced with a focus on being a soldier. I saw the transition happen. His stare shifted to sharp and he shivered, as if to shed our intimate moment in order to move to South Carolina with no regrets.

For the life of me I have no recollection of how I got home because all I remember is tears. I returned to a house of lentils and onion simmering on the stovetop and a very angry Italian mom in the doorway, ruining my moment on this wintered Earth.

"Why the hell would you go out in that? Are you crazy?" she yelled, arms flailing with a dishtowel in one hand and a wooden slotted spoon in the other.

"Maybe. I love him." I ducked under the flying arms and toward the steps, headed upstairs to my room.

"Oh please." She hit the wall under my graduation photo with the spoon. It had to have cracked. I was too tired to continue the argument, so I kept walking.

I understand as a mother now that she was being protective in a bundle of ways—frostbitten, lonesome teenager in the streets, teenage heartbreak, and frostbite, again.

He did write to me all the time. He wrote about his new army friends and how grueling boot camp was, and I wrote back about new music I loved and how much I missed him. And then I hopped on a train in April (much to my mother's chagrin), using my waitress tips to pay for the ride. We spent a weekend in Colombia, South Carolina near the fort. He made me a bath, surprised me with fresh strawberries, and we ordered a pizza in the hotel room. Sometimes young love is real. We stayed together for a little longer after he returned from boot camp.

So ... Many ... Boys ...
In All Directions ...

Safety first, that was for certain, let me make this clear—everything fell into the relationship jar, even if for two months. Intellectual connection required. I got myself tested for STDs four to six times, at least once a year in the late '90s. I was not reckless. I cared about my health. Safety girl to the point of annoying. I didn't want a baby. I didn't want an STD either.

I was so heartbroken over breaking my first love's heart at sixteen only a few years before college. Even though I knew I had to see what the fuss was about out there. In the world. And so I saw it. The fuss. I saw it from 1995 through 2001. In many shapes, colors, motorcycles, trains, avenues, towns. The first being Wintered Earth, then the flood gates opened ...

Blonds like Woody Harrelson
square jaws like Tom Cruise
art-filled hearts like mine in a Kevin Bacon face
punk haired swimmer into what was that band?
Oh yeah—MxPx.
that was a hot minute

Surfer who worked for my cousin down the shore
obsessed with waves at all hours
leaving me naked at three a.m.
because when the waves call, the surfer must listen

Actor playing opposite of me who said
he'd never let me get near a terrible guy like himself
I was too good a girl

Greek guy whose mom made me spanakopita
tall guy with son
kind guy whom I stomped all over
because he was too nice
too ready for me

Frat guy, with piano hands who began as a friend
back to Bacon
back to Tom Cruise.

Onto Songwriter guy,
old high school friend guy

I was tired
it kept me thin
all those train rides
look at me, I'm pretty

It was exciting
not one Italian guy in the bunch
I have enough in my bones for everyone
then I still felt like my first love
was communicating with me through the moon
hell bent on the love
until

The right love
The strong love
The love that
Withstands decades for reasons poets can't even capture
Love that snores and nudges and says
"Honey. Can you buzz my neck?"
"Should we buy that forest in Vermont?"

Wood Floors and Messes

A first love can be messy
and the messy memories sat in my
heart and hurt like a twisted ankle
a broken femur
for the mess I made for the person I hurt
messy mistakes
messy expression
messy and beautiful and real

I mean, we were just kids, teens
who made messes
and though I think I recall
apologies

I still left a mess in his living room
the smell of wood

and vanilla soap on his face
sad eyes, "I thought you loved me?"
"Yes, I do but we're sixteen, right?"
what a mess

But then years later, I recall
the pure love it was
before the mess
and then I think I can neaten it up in my memory
impossible
first loves are messy
and messes are forever

It's the smell of that wood
in his parents' living room
and the broken guitar on the floor
his red sweatpants
along with his broken eyes
his face full of rain

Context

He had this car. It was god-awful ugly, which made me like him more. The space-cadette-antique-loving-thrift-store-junkie I was and am, loves the things that are tossed to the side of the road. Things that have seen life. Ugly car ranks higher than polished car because it has character. Secrets. Pain and coffee stains. I didn't want nice cars. I wanted pluck. So here it was parked on campus in one of two spots. It was chocolate brown and had a wide goofy back end. When I'd spot it, all frumpy and kissing curve of the dorm parking lot, I'd reapply my lip gloss. Then I'd suck in the gut I thought I had (I had none, but I did have major body dysmorphia), and I'd find him by following the trail of cigarette smoke and his baritone laugh.

"What do you want, pretty girl?" our mutual friend "Ed" would ask when I showed up at his dorm room door propped open by a rubber band or an old pizza box. The two of them puffing and being all smug with some deluxe edition of a Beck song playing in the background. But he was hot in the Kevin Bacon sway of a way. I was all about him thinking I was the get. I still had my army boyfriend who had returned from boot camp months ago, and I still loved him, but my suspicions grew about our commitment to this relationship. Context matters, right? It's not cheating if he's cheating too. I can flirt with this guy with the ugly car, right? I don't believe these concepts now. I did then. Sort of.

"Her name is Bertha," he said and sucked in his cigarette, eyes changing between aquamarine and blue. I remember his hands being that balance of cared for and masculine that I couldn't help myself around. The hands I wanted on my hipbones that had no fat, but I thought I had layers of it. My butt was the roundest thing on my body, so why didn't I embrace it? Because it was the 1990s, that's why. In the 90s, thin was the look, and the more tired, the better. Drowned-out beauty was the ticket. Fiona Apple and Kate Moss was the heroin chic standard.

"Who?" I asked, shifting the bony hip I leaned on, sticking my smaller chest out just a bit so he sensed my barely hidden six pack. I wore bell bottom jeans and a mid-drift top like a beast.

"My car, gorgeous," he said. Then he laughed. "Bertha." Oh, the ugly piece of metal had a name. I was toast. Junk and cute.

The three of us shopped at Goodwill stores on Sundays. It was the 90s. It was glorious. Then we'd go to the diner and eat greasy food while the two of them smoked. Coffee, crispy hash browns. Chicken noodle soup in a brown and white crock. We were so New Jersey in the middle of a town in New Jersey, peppered by diners, highways, and train stations. "Ed" would tell us about how he hated his classes, actor would tell us about his upcoming auditions for shows, and I'd yammer about how I loved my professors and my new fraternity and sorority friends (but never enough to pledge or belong). We had this chemistry as a trio. But also as a duo, minus "Ed." He, God rest his beautiful soul, could not stand the chemistry between me and actor. For protective reasons. For reasons I understood then but ignored because actor was not an asshole. Or if he was, so was I, so I couldn't point fingers. And context matters, right? My boyfriend home from boot camp was most likely hanging out with other girls, I knew it deep down the way women do. So maybe this was my first lesson in self-care. Self-care wasn't a thing yet either, so I was ahead of the game. Caring for my needs. Following my crooked teenage instincts.

I do remember the first time clunky car driver and I tore each other apart, beginning with his jeans and my sundress, and I remember the thrill of never being a proper couple, and how that was part of who we were. It was probably the end of my second semester of college, and army boyfriend and I were fading fast. This new relationship had potential, until it didn't and I wanted more, but he didn't. Then fast forward to when it was reversed. Repeat. I know he thought he was too young to settle down, and I liked to act like I was too, but I probably would have been exclusive if he said the words. He had recently come out of a long-term relationship, and I was technically still in one.

During summer, spring, and winter breaks I had been working for a country market in my hometown, and that job required putting wet produce away at night. A virus got into my cuticles and caused warts on my finger. Which then spread very quickly to every finger on both hands. After many painful and unsuccessful treatments, I had lost all confidence in my appearance. I wore gloves, covered them in Vaseline and band aids, performed surgery in my dorm bathroom. I made it worse. This contributed to my overly critical habits about my body. I was all muscle because my hands were terrible. And by terrible, I mean a horror film. Everything else on me had to be tight in 1995-1996. Thighs, abs, arms, legs, and discretion about displaying my hands. I was in prison.

I hid my hands from everyone quite drastically until I was in situations where I couldn't. Blue eyes and I found ourselves in a mutual friend's dorm suite. Not our BFF who did Goodwill and diner runs. This friend was much more animated and less concerned about existential ideas and Beck. He must've had more to drink than we did because he was sound asleep in his bed with the lights on. Blue eyes and I were up and the air was very hazy with moldy carpet, cheap wood desks, and liquor.

"Show me your hands. You need to stop this. Show them to me," he said. He was gentle though. And I know why he needed to see them. Because he wanted me to stop my own madness. Break my loop. Get me outta jail.

"I caaaaan't," I said in my rum-and-coke stupor (I had two glasses, so I was drunk). "Let's skip that part, yes?" I remember doing everything I could to divert his attention to my newfound skinniness. "No hands."

"No. You have to show me. You have to love all of yourself. I will not judge you," he slurred. He meant it. I curled my fists tighter than ever. "Hands."

I cried. He comforted. I cried some more. He comforted. "I caaaan't. They're disgusting," I said. I forced my face to the disgusting carpet, knees bent into child's pose before I knew it had a name. I pressed my skull into the floor for some relief.

"They are part of you. And a temporary part. Just fuckin' show me. You will feel better. Lay your hands out flat on the carpet," he whispered. "You should not be ashamed. Rip the band aid." He sat next to me and ran his fingers through my hair, trying to find my face.

I know the way this could come across. Like he was pressuring me. But he wasn't. I remember his tone. He wanted me to be okay with all of me. And he was right. The warts wouldn't be there forever.

"FINE," I said. I laid my hands out in such painful devastation. They were massively awful. White, puffy, like rocks attached to my cuticles. I remained there—head on the filthy dorm carpet, my face red with tears and my blood buzzing with rum and coke.

"They are not so bad. You are beautiful. Come here," he said. I remember the smell of cotton sheets and my own perfume. Soap on skin. Stubble.

We put stage makeup on our passed-out friend while laughing passionately, knowing he'd laugh too if he woke up. Then, we made out for hours in the bed perpendicular to sleepy friend. We didn't have sex that night, but we learned each other's smell like animals.

The context was 1997, 1998 in peaks and valleys of whatever else was happening in my life. Fast forward to late August one of those years, both of us wasted on a cheap brand of Wheat beers. The stench of summer sweat and clove cigarettes wafting through his parents' house near my college. The chemistry of young blood. Every party-goer cried authentic tears over Princess Di's death, and we couldn't stop. Blurry night. Blurry party. Burnt lasagna in the oven. I do remember the sundress I wore though. It was maroon with pink flowers and fit my body like a glove. I can say that now because it was twenty-five years ago, and I had no idea it was beautiful then. Like I said, body dysmorphia.

Trouble is only around the corner when you write about these experiences with the blue-eyed Bertha driver in your college journal, only to realize you left that journal on your desk wide open, and your boyfriend (who's hanging on by a thread) is visiting you on a whim. You're in class across campus, and your roommate will let him in likely before you return from class. That's when you call on your other loyal friends with skills. A very specific set of skills, yes, like Liam Neeson in *Taken*. You ask this amazing male friend with the combat boots to slink into your room at light speed and remove the journal ASAP, as the clock is ticking and boyfriend is closing in on the dorm room.

Would the boyfriend have read the journal? I will never know, will I? Thank you, my friend for your loyalty and competence. This same friend also had to impersonate campus phone security as I accidentally broke into a different boy's voicemail and feared he'd miss an important voicemail about an internship he "won." I was ... restless in college, to say the least. Maybe if my boyfriend had read the journal we would've simply fallen apart a month sooner than we actually did. An earlier breakup would've spared us both some headaches and guilt.

Back to blue-eyed guy—I knew I wasn't the only girl he hung out with in the same context, but I was so cocky, despite the warts, that I didn't care. Until I did. Then he did. Then I did. And it never ever matched up. We were two vulnerable human beings who had fun while avoiding those complications that come with constant obsession over *What are we?* He was genuinely good for me at that time in my life, though I'm certain I thought he was too all over the place as it was happening, disappearing and reappearing, not belonging to any one place on campus for long.

We could talk about music, movies, whatever, for hours. He was never a jerk to me. But yet, neither of us had the energy to sort out what we were.

I think it makes you a smarter human being for things not to be so neat and tidy with people you are intimate with. Not everything needs to be established. As long as there is consent *and* respect. With those two things in place, let the fun begin— on campus, off campus, in other friends' dorm rooms while they're passed out, in his parents' room, in my dorm room, in Bertha. Casual relationships carry value if you spot it and wiggle it a bit.

Context matters: I have no shame about sowing my oats in college. In fact, I believe it makes me a better wife. I know what I have right now, and that it's built on more than attraction and chase. I have satisfaction knowing I've tried on different humans as partners. I've learned by diving into others' worlds and being naked in New Jersey, both emotionally and physically. I've been in twelve other relationships, for those who like a number. I was not a one-night-stand gal. It was enough to know for myself there's no more curiosity about sex and romance in the field. In the mountains, near the sea, wherever.

The incident on the dorm room carpet when I was challenged to show my hands was an intervention. Little did I know it would take a few doses of Interferon to get rid of the virus, but the warts disappeared eventually. Interferon is often used in cancer treatment, but it was the only one left to try. Laser and other drugs were useless. For the year I had these warts on my hand, was the year I fought with my self-image. They were big and they were a deformity of sorts. And I'm grateful someone in my life encouraged me to face it to know I wasn't what my hands were, and that I didn't have to be insecure. That experience taught me that imperfections are not the enemy.

Not every experience with love, or things like it, have the same kind of romantic smell. Some smell like oceanwater, some roses, some cigarettes, and sometimes a thing of all of those mixed together. Sometimes in ugly cars.

Femme

I'd like to study French cuisine in a chapel by myself
peeling about a literary clementine
flipping through pages made of
wood slices
as thin as
Aunt Chetti's
Eggplant
but that's so Italian

This small chapel
bellows with history
delicate lacey curtains instead of
hard stained-glass cuts.
my chapel would smell like
the patience of a New England
piemaker or
cobbler

I'd be an expert in
butter and potatoes and cheese
by hour twelve
then pray to St. Cecelia
for my voice

My in-your-face blue eyeliner
a forum
to show off my knowledge
the framework of
Feminine Crusaders L'orange
some new literary journal
me, the Editor-in-Grief

Changing Lip Colors

I can't concentrate when it's pink
only brown gives me life
sparkly nudes and
hungry sandstones set it off

Pink makes me tired
like a weary food-shopper who
hasn't slept in months because insomnia loves
to grab her like the arcade claw

Give me brown lipstick
Give me Life
Give me 1997

Boys Club

The stink of
boys on my right side
filled my nostrils
sing it
she sang it: Tori Amos sang it
then she sacrificed them to a volcano of sorts
but instead of stealing her words
I'll push mine to the northeast

The burdock flower urges me to
be wary of
an offer
to purify the air in my house and
think on it
not to surrender to
praise that smells like

the pain in the
summer
sordid

Instead, follow the protection of the
purple burdock rising in
September.
its prickly fingers
steeping in sweetness
fighting
The stink of

male fear
ego, and
routine

"Oh but they're such nice boys"

Are they?

ELAINA BATTISTA-PARSONS

The Emerald

He was a cross between Tom Cruise and Christian Bale. I mean. He spoke five languages, played classical piano, and fenced competitively. He was nothing like anyone I had dated at my private university, not to say the guy with the six-inch spiked bleached hair from the swim team wasn't on fire, but still. Those guys were athletic and outgoing, and if they were cake they'd be funfetti with vanilla icing. This guy was Renaissance and full of literature: deep chocolate imported from France with an icing made of fresh mint crushed in one of those mortar and pestle things. Art and history swam through his veins, and you could see it in the way he laughed and in his clean hands. His fingers were manicured without being feminine. The hand thing again.

He went to the Ivy League school only twenty minutes around the corner—an Ivy League in the middle of a charming old town with chapels dotting every corner. He studied economics on a level beyond anything my school could handle. We met at a chain restaurant one snowy evening over winter break. Neutral ground against a basket of ribs, fries, and sodas. I wasn't drinking age yet. Neither was he so he sipped on seltzer.

We both had a friend with us that twelve-degree December night. His friend was the plainest guy on the East Coast with a penchant for physics and mine was a gorgeous and talented friend from school.

We arrived to an almost empty TGI Fridays which was both a relief, but also kind of a bummer. I was somewhere between starving and bored. Then I saw that jawline and the eyes. I smiled at him from across the empty floor of the bleach-smelling chain restaurant—my face landed on his jaw at his four-top as he and his friend talked loudly, but still seemed as bored as me. They sucked the buffalo sauce from their index fingers while simultaneously checking us out with demonstrative side eye. *Ahh. Non-Ivy League girls looking for fun.* But really, I just wanted to pig out. And whether or not they knew we weren't from their university, I'm just speculating. Do Ivy League girls have an essence? I do not know.

We sat at tables with only a walkway to the kitchen separating us. The night was late December and quiet, when all you want is French fries covered in cheese and chicken fingers because no one will see you naked but yourself in the next two days ... or at least that's what you think when you plan this icy-road outing. The holidays were over and I had maybe two days left until resolutions should commence.

Despite my full Italian roots and a dollop of Spain, some people mistook me for being Irish. "You don't look Italian," he said later that night. He touched one of the curls on my shoulder and I was finished. "You're exquisite."

You had to fulfill certain requirements for me to love you from ages eighteen to twenty-two. If you didn't meet these standards, I probably wouldn't stay interested for long, but if you met most, I'd be yours for as long as you adored my thin waist and purple lip gloss. Pompous? Absolutely. Do I still live my life this way? Absolutely not. He met the requirements. He was hardworking, glittery eyed, left-handed, non-Italian-looking (and smelling), funny, had an IQ that fit a gifted and talented student, and obsessed with music as much as I was. He able to have an hour-long conversation about one song. When I say requirements, there was always wiggle room, except in the music category.

"Where do you girls go to school?" he asked, breaking the ice and the tension. Someone had to speak first.

"Around the corner. How about you?" I asked and recognized that I was slouching, so I bolted upright. My friend gave me eyes that were full of mixed signals.

"The same." I knew where he meant. "Around the corner, and past a flower garden, though now it's covered in snow." He sipped his drink and shot eyes at me that may as well have unsnapped my bra.

His skin was more flawless than mine and his physique, slightly more defined in his black turtleneck and jeans. I was up for the challenge. God, I was vain at twenty. To put it kindly.

After cozying up with them in their booth at that chain restaurant, learning the basics of their personalities, barely knowing their names, we took them back to the dorm suite I was staying in over winter break. I had a role in *Lend Me a Tenor* that opened in February, so they offered rooms to the cast to make getting to rehearsals easier. It had a U-shaped common room. That's where my friend and his friend hung out and watched some old rom com DVD left from the original occupants of the suite.

Fencer and I made out in the room next door. It was moonlit, strange, and extremely satisfying. I was kissing a really clean stranger who I brought home. This was a first. The stranger part, not the clean. They left at dawn.

"Do we really need to go anywhere?" my friend had asked me only hours ago, as she applied the last of her nude lipstick. "It's freezing out."

"No. But let's go anyway. I want wings and soda until my jean button pops," I answered. I checked my body profile a million times before shutting off the lights and leaving my temporary housing for the TGI Fridays on the highway between my school and his.

We dated for a few months after that. My friend and his friend lasted a couple weeks. Our favorite thing to do was hang out in his room and order pizza, in his historical dorm building where famous authors and their friends studied, dipped their quills in ink, and drank "spirits." I picked up extra shifts at a local pizzeria so that I could afford the extra gas required to make those forty-minute round trips into town to see him every other day or night. My friendships were tossed to the side of the road. God, twenty was awfully special.

I was more than excited at the idea of his face and his hands being all for me. Someone this attractive was a win, and now a conquest to keep. Dating typical college guys with typical athleticism and solid biceps was getting monotonous. I stood up straighter around him. He challenged me to drop even a couple more pounds and to be a smidge hotter. At first, this bugged me, but he claimed I'd be even healthier. Whether I believed him or not, I lived in that space. He admitted to not having the most nurturing family growing up, so maybe I needed to show him that extra support. Right? Isn't that what good girlfriends do? I could still call myself a feminist, right?

Our fourth or fifth "date" was out of a 1920s novel. We walked around his Ivy League campus doused in wild lilies and purple peonies. The architecture on campus struck a mood. We held hands and looked "in love." That night, I happened to be wearing an olive-green corduroy skirt, matching tights, and a bright red lip, while he wore a long black winter coat and carried sheet music in a briefcase. We were a portrait of vintage. Posters about an alternative punk band competition decorated every black light pole, reminding me it was really 1998. Chapel bells sang. I met his Ivy League friends at every new brick path and curve of the campus. Wow. A lot of female Ivy League friends. And every guy was more handsome than the last. But I knew he'd never be able to take his hands off me as long as my waist was the way it was and my eyes outlined in dark brown. He loved the fire behind them, unable to tell if I was faking fire or not.

We stood in the flower garden on campus and kissed for twenty minutes, inhaling each other's evil and good. I would keep him interested, even if it meant more shifts for gas money and less sleep. Even if it meant jogging until I couldn't feel my legs.

"Can you give me a ride to the airport with my car?" I asked him, as I was chosen to interview in Los Angeles for a paid summer internship with Nissan USA.

"Can I use your car while you're away, gorgeous?" He negotiated. I didn't care.

The morning of my flight, upon arrival at Philadelphia International Airport, he dug his thumb into my hips with desperation. He tugged me closer to lick behind my ear in the middle of the airport parking lot. We did our dance in that lot. All couples have a dance that doesn't resemble anything like an actual dance, but more of an affection session. He smelled like triumph if it had a smell, and I would never go back to sort-of smart guys. Who cares that my friends spotted his cockiness from miles away. They called him Chip Ivy. They didn't approve. But I approved of the way I had to practice so much restraint to not tear him apart in that parking lot.

"When I asked him if he was a fencer, he said, 'I fence. I'm not a fencer,'" my best friend told me.

"Give him a chance. He's sweet," I said. Then I'd shift my weight from leg to leg, unable to grip the Earth because of the pounds of muddy crap falling out of my mouth. It's so funny how aware of the bullshit narratives we tell ourselves, but can't always put an end to them.

I wanted Ivy League's smell on me day and night. He gave my body things that no other guy had yet. I wasn't a virgin by any means, but he did it like Tom Cruise did in *Top Gun*. I mean, he did resemble him, after all. Disapproving friends. Great Sex. What would you choose at twenty?

"No worries. I'll give your car back in one piece when you come back, beautiful," he told me. Then he ran his nose up my cheek one more time with the choreography of a fencer who went to an Ivy League school.

I landed in LA later in the evening after a pleasant four-hour flight from Philadelphia International, the most convenient one from my college campus and his dorm only twenty minutes from there. LA was a nice welcome, as I left a rainy, cool spring behind and entered a summery sweet evening on the west coast near Hermosa Beach, CA. Nissan USA put me up in a luxurious hotel for the interview process which was more than I could have imagined as a college student who struggled to pay her car insurance monthly from waitress tips. I'd enjoy the amenities of LA for two days. I missed his hands all over me, but I'd suck in the sunshine and breeze from the other ocean.

In my interview group at the hotel were college juniors from all over the country. I was immediately drawn to a brawny Texan named Josh. He spoke more vibrantly in my presence. I knew that because

I watched the group from across the room before I joined them at the round table in the lobby. The girls were very friendly—one from Minnesota named Janis, and Holly from Maryland. I only wanted to chat with Josh though. He was a guy, and he was eyeing me up and down. My extra sit ups paid off every time. So did my mascara wand.

We ended up breaking away from the group and had dinner on Nissan's bill because that was included in our interview "package." I ordered grilled shrimp over romaine with fennel, while Josh ate a 16 oz sirloin and roasted red potatoes. We had a lot in common, as we were both college juniors with all kinds of lofty career goals in advertising.

I noticed Josh's rough hands and eager eyes, almost trying to ignore his very thick Texan accent. It just didn't sing truth to my Jersey ear, but his biceps made up for it, under his perfectly fit plaid shirt. Twenty was vain and warped. The hotel restaurant was nicer than anywhere I had eaten in the past couple of years.

"Do you have a boyfriend back home?" Josh asked as me as he sipped his seltzer with lime. He pushed his straw to the side of the glass when he did it.

"Yes. But he's back home, you know?" I answered, and sliced a piece of extra thick fennel covered in lemon and oil. My eyes found his so he knew what I implied.

"I do know. I have a girlfriend." He sliced his steak without looking at it, as if to say, I know where I want this to go. Also that he ate meat as a lifestyle.

We talked and droned on about our lives back home, then some dessert flirtation, until finally we had an opening to do whatever we pleased. Josh extended his hand for me to join him on the balcony overlooking the LA sunset. It was a true California view with a warm breeze that reeked of French kisses and gut-tingling vibes. We both felt it and inched closer. Josh reached around me to subtly grab my waist to let me know he was game

But I couldn't. I wasn't a cheater, really. I missed Chip Ivy. "I'm sorry. I can't. But listen, good luck tomorrow at the interview."

He looked surprised, of course. He stepped closer to me thinking he could change my mind if the breeze blew in the smell of his skin.

"Really? We're thousands of miles away from home," he said. I was reconsidering when I looked at his shoulders. The way he towered over me.

"I know. I'm not great at cheating. I'm sorry." I wiped my forehead and fought away some nausea. I gripped his bicep accidentally, or maybe not. That I can't recall.

"Okaaay. Well, then, bye." He grazed my hand with his, and left the balcony.

I never saw him again. If he fought a little harder I may have given in.

I slipped back to my own hotel room, turned on reruns of *Three's Company* and tried to call his dorm from the hotel phone. No one answered, so for sure he had a fencing meet. He never really talked about what he'd be doing while I was away. I hung up the hotel phone and momentarily regretted my decision to reject Josh. Instead of doing anything about it, I shut off the light and fell asleep before midnight.

Exactly three days later, back on the Ivy League campus and happy to be home from LA, I secured my hand in his. My twenty-first birthday arrived. I pleaded with my boss to have the Friday off from work. To be with him. We walked across the campus like dates prior, but today he was walking faster and with a silent frustration. Even his arm swing felt irate.

"Sorry. My math sets were difficult, I got a B on my Lit paper, and my mom is giving me crap about not coming home for February break next week," he told me. "Even though she could care less when I am actually home." He flicked the bark of the oak tree behind him, clearly nervous about the conversation.

"No worries. Let's just enjoy the rest of my birthday," I said and grabbed his face in mine to look him flat in the eyes.

His eyes refused to meet mine. I tried harder by grabbing him over his pants, thinking I'd get the usual grunt from him where he then cannot keep his eyes, hands, or face away from me. Where he'd be as close to me as humanly possible and my nerve endings between my legs took over and we'd both give in. It wasn't working, and it was driving me batty. I even snuck an extra coat of lip gloss on my mouth, thinking that would make him notice.

"Not now … I'm just … I'm not in the mood," he was now attempting to pull off an entire chunk of the oak's bark like it was an assignment. I grabbed his free hand and held it like I meant it.

"What did you do while I was gone? I really missed you," I changed the subject with an air of lightness.

I knew what was happening, but I knew how to hang on to every shred of a relationship. A talent. A curse. Whichever.

"I drove around a little bit. But mostly stayed on campus for a party or two. Had a fencing meet. Nothing exciting." He dropped my hand and tossed the freed bark into a grassy courtyard.

We walked toward his dorm room. He had both hands in his pockets and left me inches behind him. "How was LA? Did you hook up?" His eyes bowed to the ground.

"Hook up? You know ... I almost did. But then you. I thought of you," I said deflated as I raced to be in step with him. He opened his dorm room door with the dog tag-shaped key and tossed his things onto the top bed of the bunk. The smell of pine filled my nose. New soap. "Wait, you would have been okay if I kissed someone else?" I asked. I ripped off my coat and straddled him as he sat at his desk chair facing out the window. Shreds.

"No. I am glad you didn't. But I get it if you did, you know?" he said with scrunched Tom Cruise eyebrows. He pulled out some Chapstick and put it all over his lips too many times.

"No. I don't know," I said and removed myself from his hard crotch and thighs of iron.

"Listen, gorgeous. Let me give you your gift. I have been excited about it all day. It's under that scarf." He motioned to the bottom bed of his bunk.

All I could imagine was something like a necklace or a bracelet with my initials engraved. He definitely could afford it. Five languages, classical piano, and fencing. Come on.

I giggled and kissed his neck, forgetting all about anything else leading up to this. He had to have been in love. He just had a bad day is all.

"I put a lot of thought into your gift. I need you to love it," he said with his fingertips touching the other set of fingertips in a triangle.

"I'm sure I will," I answered and gave him a warm tongue-filled kiss and shoved my hand down his pants playfully, back out again. I approached the scarf-covered gift with high expectations.

Under the Ivy League school scarf was a tag labeled *The Emerald*. The box was rectangular and twelve inches long. Inside the box was an emerald green soft plastic vibrator. I'm pretty sure my heart stopped.

"You know. For when I'm not around. I hope you like it," he said. He sat back in his desk chair pleased with himself, leaning is head in his hands. "Want to order pizza?"

"I … I …" I couldn't find the words. In fact, even if I could, they'd spill out in salt and bile.

I hugged him, hoping to squeeze the bullshit out of him, holding in every emotion. We exchanged pleasantries about the gift, and I said I'd see him in a couple days. My face hit the February air and my eyes focused on the brick path that led to the parking lot across the street. The campus felt blank. The flowers still seemed full of themselves, the air full of snow and silence. Once out of sight, I let the tears gush as I opened my car door. My car smelled like lilac perfume. I hadn't noticed it when he picked me up from the airport. I threw The Emerald into my backseat and drove back to my dorm. But not before stopping for a chocolate donut and a large vanilla cone with all the sprinkles they had.

Tre

Forza

Strength

Strong Legs

I really love my strong legs. They earned me first and second place in elementary school for the running long jump two years in a row, beating boys with big biceps who wore cologne in fifth grade. My legs paved my years as an athlete and dancer. Later, they helped me deliver my babies vaginally, and more recently, allowed me to get out of the hospital fairly quickly after a bilateral mastectomy and DIEP-flap reconstruction.

"Look at you, show off," my surgeon remarked with his team of interns behind him. At this point he wore jeans and sweatshirt, seventy-two hours after he remade my breasts, utilizing fat from my belly. He molded B-cup meatball-sized breasts. This required reattaching blood vessels tinier than most things we can imagine. My legs pushed me across the shiny marble of the recovery floor twice, only hours after I'd been rebuilt. The baby cancer nodules were tossed into the trash, alongside my female glands that were trying to kill me. If that sounds offensive and harsh, I don't know what to tell you. Breast cancer has no mercy and that offends me more. Two laps around the nurse's station hunched over, but I did it because I wanted to get home and eat ice cream in my motorized recliner that other mastectomy-reconstruction patients used for recovery. The recliner being a rite of passage. A symbol that I did it. I wanted to heal with *The Golden Girls* and feel-good movies.

My mom has strong legs too. My dad, brother. Strong, able legs from thigh to ankle. I remember as a kid always staring down at my legs as I touched my toes before I stepped into the shower, thinking—my legs are full of muscles, and I like them. Imagine if we could keep that kind of self-love stirring through the years? For my legs, I have. In leg years, I'm still eight. They drag me across the beach when both arms are weighed down by wet towels, clumsy umbrellas, and sand-filled buckets. They pulled me out of bed in the ICU when the rest of my body from the lower pelvic region up was highly stitched and freshly closed up. They caught my dog when he ran away the first week we had him. They never gave up on two vaginal births when they were required to help me bear down for my life. Pain. Criminal. Expel.

I refuse to let my legs turn to mush. I notice my mom's legs are still strong at age seventy-four, so perhaps there is hope to keep them fierce and in charge of my years left on Earth. I should mention that my mother's legs are a result of her constant moving. Walking. Kitchen-conquering. Nervous-energy-house-scrubbing. When I wake up every morning, I promise my legs I won't grow tired. Even if I want a lazy day or two, or three, I reassure them that I'll work them harder tomorrow.

You know those offensively hot days of July or August when you have kids and you're in an amusement park that you should've left an hour or more ago, but they insisted on every roller coaster? That's when strong legs come in handy. Because then at least your feet can thank them for the support, and they were spared a tad more. All you want is a cold drink and some shade and maybe fries, but strong legs keep you going and make you feel like your heart can do it too. In those moments of summer weariness, I always think to myself, "I'm going to train for a marathon. My legs can do that." Then I remember when I start jogging too long that my lungs are also involved.

Think about a seated life. Think about life without stride, pointed toe, accentuated thigh muscle, bent knee, foot to gravelly pavement. Legs are a privilege, a gift. To those who can't use theirs, I imagine they'd say to us who can: "Do it. Use them." To keep them pumping, breathing, flexing to nourish. Thigh muscles are royalty and home to a fluffy pup on a cold, January night. Your flight from ghastly sights, like loveless fields of right/red/fake-fact nonsense. Run the fight of your life.

Our legs take us to places where we spill our feelings over coffee and oatmeal in small downtowns. Legs drag us to tables for spare ribs and whiskey, and they get us home on purple August evenings after shrimp and lemonade. Days when the sun drained us gloriously or holly covered snow piles wore us out before stew and warmth. Legs seem to be queen of the whole.

Stretch out like a lover who means it
hamstrings tighter than a bra strap
legs only work when worked
even when all you want is a book and a mug of ice cream
because often I want a book and ice cream
leaving my legs to wait until morning
to be extended, mended, and totally
in control

ELAINA BATTISTA-PARSONS

My Doc Martens Sound like
Chrissy Hynde
When They Speak

I didn't mean to begin a collection of Doc (Dr.) Martens in my house. It sort of happened naturally. My oldest daughter has that same spiral of rebel and drums raining in her head. All around her. For now, at least. The spiral could be a phase, or like her mother, a protest embedded in her pulse. Together we lace up, stomp, and rule the world. One outing at a time. One Pride Day, one ice cream run, one day at a time.

Growing up, I got to hear all about how my taste in shoes was less than feminine, and it occurred to me that maybe it was me that wasn't so feminine.

Turns out I was simply too young and inexperienced in life to understand that wasn't the case at all. I am both feminine and masculine, with a little bit of everything in between. Lipstick-phile with a case of The Smiths. A cis-straight woman who loves all kinds of things, vintage, new, and then right back round again. But, still, my shoes are never feminine. My pretty knee-high riding boots barely make the cut. A pointy shoe means death for my inner Dolores O'Roirdan. God, that one hurt.

Enter my Doc Martens who sound like Chrissy Hynde when they speak. I even recorded a conversation between them and the March-soaked ground.

Docs: Good things happen with hard work. This day is mine for the win.

Ground: Oh but beware of the people who don't love a confident girl. They'll spit sludge in your direction, raspy-voiced one. Step carefully. Be gentle. Tame the flame a little. Throw sand on the fire a bit.

Docs: Change for them? Fuck that. I mean no harm. I want us all to succeed.

Ground: They won't believe you.

Docs: Should I care?

Ground: I mean...beware of the rattlesnakes.

Especially the childhood ones who really

don't want you to do well. That makes them really squirmy.

Docs: I'll stomp them in their tracks. Besides they can do well, too right?

Ground: Not in they're in their own way. They slither and climb

around poles and trees

and hide in these vicious parts. Between the boards.

Docs: I'll take my chances.

Ground: No shit. But my advice: don't be so predictable.

Surprise them with kindness.

Docs: Of course.

Ground: Still with boundaries. It's a tricky tango.

Docs: You have a lot to say for a chunk of concrete.

Ground: Not everything is as seems, Doc.

Docs are persistent. I'm proud of their bravery, even though I know the ground is

looking out for them. The ground has their best interest in mind, but my Docs don't

budge in their courage, and that's commendable. It makes me feel worthy of their wear.

Chosen, almost.

As my Docs and the ground end this conversation in the parking lot of my favorite coffee shop, I get an email on my phone from Doc Martens the business, saying "Wear your Heart on Your Docs."

I can do better, Dr. Marten, LLC.
Mine speak in the voice of The Pretenders' Chrissy Hynde.
Raspy,
Well-Meaning quips,
The only thing they pretend to be is patient.

Music-Eater

"I listen to all kinds of music. I love it all. One day I will listen to classical, the next, hip-hop," say the music lovers. That is fine and respectable. But do you eat it and taste it, and die without it? Do you sweat and panic and wrangle your brain cells and itch like crazy until you find the exact song you need in that exact moment ... then feel your heart, breath, and pulse even out once the intro slams into your ears? Do you frantically search for that title that will feed you? That's the difference between the eaters and the "I love all music" tribe.

I have lunch with friends. We eat outside overlooking the river, and a live cover band is playing a setlist mostly composed of popular 1980s hits. Great hits. Everything from Pat Benatar to The Clash to Fleetwood Mac. They cover every genre within the decade, hit the notes, and entertain the diners. But my lord, as soon as we finish our afternoon together, and I start my car, if I don't find The Kooks' song called "Sway," I might never get rid of this sort of headache that started from too much stimulus. I might not get rid of the feeling that I really didn't relate to much of what the vibe was at the restaurant. It was too happy. Too beach-town. Too … American. I need the Kooks' UK snark ASAP. (This is how music-eaters operate.)

I am not saying one group of "musicologists" is superior to the other, I am simply saying there is a difference between loving, rocking, singing to your beloved songs while you drive versus not being able to fully function and regulate your blood pressure until you hear the bridge you need to hear at any given moment. Or the key change that gives your backbone an adjustment. The stuff that cracks your neck and cools you down. My husband and I are this way. It's a critical part of our life's itinerary. Our existence. Our daily function. The way we succeed as people in the world.

And I know there are millions like us. The surgeons and the eaters and the disciples of the music born from a very innate place. It's like a cleanse sometimes too—after a stressful day or meeting or encounter. Or after a day listening to someone else's country pop or Post Malone playlist. It's urgent and it's primal when you're an eater. And you will be called a music snob, but hey. There are worse things. I assume the eaters are almost always musicians themselves, (not tinkerers). I played the flute and the baritone horn, and reading music was very challenging for me, but it changed how I experienced music, for sure. Actual readers and graspers of scale and melody. That would explain the surgical scrutiny of every line and lyric. The ones that send us through the roof, and into heaven while still tasting the salty ocean. Let me provide my best example: "Father Lucifer" by Tori Amos.

The intro adjusts my breath. Like I'm entering the most beautiful cemetery in June: deep and even. The verse makes me feel sleepy in a good way. Same with verse two. But that bridge. I usually "rewind" the bridge twice. There's so much to hear and feel and eat. And I want the full experience every time. And if someone in my car is talking during it, I have to restart that bridge. She triple layers her vocals. And every layer is like cake icing. Three separate messages. Three separate flavors. It's so spiritual.

It's wonderful that everyone can enjoy and love all kinds of music. But do you eat it, digest it, and repeat the cycle because you clench it so tightly in your bones and vital organs, and it's become part of your physiology?

Veal over Polenta

My immensely beautiful and super tiny Italian grandma used to slow cook a veal chop on the bone in a pan on her gas stove. In oil, garlic, and parsley for hours, using nothing but a fork to nudge and flip, and her instinct to know when it had enough heat. Usually by hour three it had been slowly cooked to the point of gently trickling off the bone and into my nineteen-year-old mouth after months of eating mostly bland salads, Lucky Charms, and gummy peaches from the university snack store.

Sometimes she'd stir up some polenta to have with the veal. A sprinkle of parmesan over the velvet sunshine. We'd listen to Julio Iglesias or Andrea Bocelli and she'd smile watching me eat. I can still smell her soft skin and see her crooked fingers as she dipped the plain cookie in her afternoon coffee. Yola Ricci.

We'd sit in her north Jersey apartment kitchen and she'd tell me how happy in love I'd be someday and how I'd love my babies to no end. To no understanding. To no limit. Under every condition. I miss her terribly. We were best friends. Particularly the years that I had no idea about anything.

I remember visiting her during every spring or winter break I had while in college—when I was trying to figure out where my life was headed after graduation. She'd hold my hand at the kitchen table and smile. She was so proud of me. "You'll be successful," she'd say. She'd ask about my love life, and I'd tell her that I met nice people and made amazing friends. "You will have smart, beautiful babies. And you will be a good mother like your mother." Then when I married my second and permanent husband, I'd visit with my first daughter on a random Saturday or weekday. She'd watch my daughter play and admire her figurines on the end tables. "Does she love her father too, Elaina?" She always said my name. I'd tell her how close she was with her dad, and that made her so happy. I know there were generational nuances in her questions. She was curious about relationships and human nature. My grandma was an expert in love and compassion.

Her hands
bony and veiny
rings loose, nails rose pink and brittle
her hands
in mine
forever
to the tune of the rosary

The Newark Bedroom

I was there, I swear. In my white- and blue-speckled hospital gown, flesh freezing from the open window, in between my Grandma Yola and Aunt Norma. Soft skin, Italian gaze, buttoned up in jewel tone winter coats and silk scarves tied around their chins. Exactly the way I remembered them best. Women who knew things about toxic masculinity before it had a name, and likely too polite to ever express their frustration about it. Well, Gram at least. I was a lead actress in this hospital dream with raw stiches, oily wavy hair, and a thirsty mouth that spoke only as needed.

They were looking in my eyes, hands on my bruised arms, telling me I was okay. I'd been rolled into recovery from the ICU twelve hours prior. Yet here I was, lying in my Grandma's queen bed, aluminum closets on both sides, and the enormous kitchen only a door away, in Newark, NJ. I was initially terrified that they had arrived to take me with them. And then shortly at ease to know they were probably interested in only revealing that I was doing great. I could smell the Stella Doro cookies dipped in coffee on the kitchen table.

I wanted to say, "Why are your coats on?" but deep down I knew they probably had just bought escarole and saltines from the local market. This had to be a dream. A dream with cheap Italian cookie smells.

My nurses told me to take it easy, and to call for help to use the restroom. I was stitched up from hip to hip from where they grabbed my belly fat to make me new B cups, and then stitches around each new breast from the mastectomy. Four drains in my body and hanging from various openings, wires situated in my gown pockets. My entire torso was compromised, but my legs and arms weren't. I didn't call the nurses. I drank tiny pink pitcher after tiny pink pitcher of ice water. Okay, so I did call them for one reason. When it comes to flushing, I go to extremes. Pitcher after pitcher I guzzled.

Every fifteen minutes I got up to pee, with no nurse's help, because A. I was forty-two and strong as hell and B. I didn't want to bother them. They had enough work to do between checking my temperature every half hour, emptying my drains every few hours, and listening to the "heartbeat" of my new breasts, making sure every nerve and atom was melding and connecting in a way that would keep them alive. If they turned the wrong color, I'd have to be wheeled back into surgery. I hit a point where I just needed to breathe and relax. Give myself a minute. Allow the Italian-ladies-in-scarves dream to unfold.

I got more than I anticipated. Who knows if it was the extreme amount of Tylenol and drugs they were pumping into my system, or my delirium from not having slept for real in days, but I felt my ancestors. I felt my beloved grandmother and her sister next to me. I heard their voices, smelled their winter coats. The silk of their head scarves that smelled like fresh lipstick. I lay still. Breathe ... I don't remember what they said to me. Their presence was magnetic. I like to believe they were there to remind me that in this moment of vulnerability and depletion, I was doing what generations of women before me have— healing in whatever way I saw fit for me. For me, that meant moving

So, I sat up, hyperventilated, and wailed for the first time since getting out of surgery three days prior. I heave-cried, no matter how much it hurt my raw stitches.

The nurse came into my room and placed her hand on my back. Her eyes felt soft. "This is very normal. It's okay. You're okay. You did it." And she rubbed my back.

I told her about my visit. She told me she believed me. She probably had to say that. After letting out the last of my sobs, I lowered myself back down, and closed my eyes. I think I napped for ten minutes. The windows were wide open—because I insisted, as cold as it was that April weekend. The staff commented that it felt like Denver in my room. I told them I needed the cold air to feel better.

This particular hospital was a teaching hospital in NJ, and I cannot say enough excellent things about their staff. Every single one of them. From the caretaker who bathed me because I begged for a shower. To the amazing Russian male nurse who made me laugh because he said my breast pulses sounded like a spaceship landing. I hope he fell in love by now. Any guy would be so lucky to have him. I wish I could find him now and be his friend. He had that certain quality we all want in friends—honesty.

The visit, the cry. That had to be a dream. The next day I felt new. I still had barely slept a wink, but something about my existence felt vivid, and like I was going home soon. I wanted ice cream. And a roast beef sub when I got home. *Ghostbusters* was on TV on my wall, so I watched with a sense of I'm totally going home. I still couldn't look at my surgical work, but I knew the work felt tight, precise, and done with so much experience. I forever thank science and medicine for their work in the world. Good surgeons are artists and ultimate humanitarians.

I went home that day after my final visits with my surgeons who were extra pleased with my progress in the span of four days. I didn't dare tell them that my late grandmother and aunt came by, and that was part of why I felt recharged and ready to go home.

If I focus and close my eyes, I can still go back to that bedroom in the Newark house that my grandma rented for years. If I sauté some garlic in oil, the travel is even brighter. The kitchen was the center of that house, and the bedrooms lined the sides. She'd make my brother and me wagon wheel macaroni and take us to the local Italian market, called Prosperity, for candy of our choice. I can jump into the dream in an instant.

We can filter in what brings us toward healing.
Ancestors, memories, belief in our bodies, whatever
it may be. Dream compositions starring flutes over
violins. Drums over bass. Oboe inside melody.

Nobody tells you about that bedroom-in-Newark
dream state before you get rolled into surgery for
twelve hours. And I'm kind of glad they don't. I
preferred the surprise and the precise timing.

Healing requires more than vitamins and meds
a thick layer of *I want to be* well and
I want to run faster

out there under the moon

don't tell the person undergoing treatment
I'm Sorry
tell them,
You are strong. You can fight
reminding them they have this

They don't want your apologies
they want your push

Dishtowel

My mother had a dishtowel
that smelled like
hustle.

Years of hustle
all moms have a smell only their child knows

And hers was soaked in the dishtowel
a cross between parsley garnished hustle
and fresh flowers

That dishtowel was often
swung over her shoulder
in a choreography of gumption
and Italian mom omniscience

Gold Jewelry, We're Rich

It must've been about 1988 when my mom met Susan. Susan loved birds for pets, and jewelry. Mostly the fourteen-karat gold kind with colorful stones fastened into their brackets. Gold that dangled, gold that twinkled. Susan and her jewelry were the epitome of beach town glamour. I was eleven, but I saw it. Susan bought "special" pieces from a vendor in New York City, then hired people like my mom to sell them on the Jersey Shore. And yes, there was a market for it—friends, families, come look at the shiny things and buy all of the jewelry. Collect. Mingle. Twirl it in your manicured gemstone-matching nails.

I'd go with my mom to Susan's house every few Saturdays on a late morning and we'd sit and ooh and ahh Susan's new purchases from her vendor.

"Corinna," she says to my mom. "These are really pretty. And so popular now. You might want to grab a few in different colors," Susan would insist, with her peach manicure and blue macaw, Maggie, on her shoulder.

I thought *Wow. My mom will have so much money to buy more jewelry. More manicures. More shoes.* Whatever. In addition to her full-time job, she'd have more salary. This was good for us because sometimes I heard my parents stress about the washer and dryer costing money to fix. Or how Finley Fuel raised their prices.

Often, Susan provided gold chains with various kinds of links, sometimes rose gold. I learned the difference among golds that year: yellow, rose, and white. I learned about different chain lengths too. Sometimes Susan had rings with chunky stones. The most popular item was the people. Their midsection made of stone like topaz or garnet, and the legs dangled in three miniscule gold beads. The head was a gemstone too, sometimes matching the body, sometimes not. Can you imagine a grandmother opening this box on Mother's Day with her grandkids and their birthstones? This is what it was about in my shore town of New Jersey in the late eighties.

ELAINA BATTISTA-PARSONS

Gold glistening on overly tan bosoms on the beach and at backyard summer parties. Oh Joyce, I looove your necklaces. Where did you get them? The more glitz, the better. It matched their cigarette smoke. Lemonade, potato chips, and cigarettes.

Susan also sold specialty pendants, in the shape of her beloved macaw parrots, crosses, initials, and probably things I'm forgetting. I was a big fan of silver in my teenage years, so anything with silver and black stones was my style. She sold those too. And my mom was one of the lucky sales gals who got to make lots of extra money, I'd think.

"Corinna, wait until you see the gorgeous new bracelets I just got."

Here's what selling the jewelry looked like to me as a pre-teen, then a teen, because I'm pretty sure this side gig with Susan lasted until 1991 when I was thirteen or fourteen. We'd sit and let Susan model the inventory on that Saturday. We'd leave with a decent inventory of gold and stones, all zipped tightly in their clear mini bags, snapped airtight. That was part of the fun. Price tags included. Someone (usually my mom) would host a jewelry party on her dining room table on random Saturdays or Sundays. Family and friends would browse, eat, buy a few items, and my mom would get a percentage of the sales. I thought it was fun and exciting. Mom had extra cash.

It was very natural for my mom do this on the side, as she has always been the person with the prettiest jewelry. The stylish one. The one with the two-year New York fashion school background that she never had a chance to see through completely. It made sense. Susan had the right girl. And I remember my mom toting around the inventory when we'd visit family on holidays or dinners. She kept it in a soft black travel tote. I enjoyed the ritual of unzipping the clear bags and displaying the jewelry on a table. I got to know the pieces and even owned a few. My favorites were the bright green emerald-ish stones and the thick silver chains ending in an onyx rectangle pendant. Maybe I'd be like Susan one day.

I didn't know then that those shiny gold chains and pendants paid for things my brother and I needed, like uniforms and dance costumes. I didn't know then that, though my mom enjoyed the parties and toting the bag around, it was more essential than extra. I didn't know that finding Susan was the difference between being able to pay the dance competition fee or decline if my class qualified that year. I didn't know then that the commission paid for my brother's better pair of soccer cleats. I didn't know a lot of things. I knew we always had the prettiest necks and wrists in town.

Snow Lover

Suspended in air, origin water, destination hearth and home. Winter is the answer to everything. You can hide and refresh. Reboot in the coolness of your pillow, coffee in hand, *Family Stone* on the TV. Dinners feel more eventful when it's dark outside. Days blend into nights and nights cleanse the playground slides and turf with frozen, invisible mops. The sound of snow falling is like your loved ones forgiving you. And you, the same. Winter is the explosion of grace. Forgiveness, the novella.

Snow begins with a scent. Then a shiver. Late night snows electrify your being because the next morning is extended, and you know it. Cars stuck. Coffee bubbles. Weather reports sing. Pause. All is on pause. If you have to drive, my deepest apologies. I mean that.

I always imagine how beautiful it would be to light a few candles in the snow, just above the snow crust— black, white, maybe a dark purple candle. Neighbors would call the cops I'm sure, in my town. Winter witch! Winter witch! Weird, Strange! Blah! Blah! Zero imagination around here. There's always the backyard, I suppose, but what if I want to somehow bless, celebrate, and conjure up things in the front of my home? What if I wanted to let the trees know they look even better with no leaves and a white set of teeth?

Peppermint
breath
January aftertaste
I imagine snow as my companion
then return to my
quiet whiskey and clove under blankets
with the people I love
The thing with snow, though
is that against its clean canvas, not much can be hidden

Facts and fights shine like ornaments
pain is louder in the cold
still
snow is the loyalest of flakes

ELAINA BATTISTA-PARSONS

The night walks after a snow
speak comfort,
placidity
a vibration that feels like
concerts of violin and rose gold harps

Vene Italiana (Italian veins)

The shallot requires razor-thin precision, but the bread …
break bread all over my face
rip it, dip it
garlic-rubbed olive oil on our cuticles for days
soapy sponge in circles all over the dirty sink
our forearms veiny and Italian
for days our hands bleed a chap that screams God

Holy Mary, Mother of *God*
an extra chemical in female Italiana
perhaps a code of DNA that's encrypted
to move like our curly life and pasta depend on it
every wipe, tickling the countertop
NO SPOTS! God's watching
she knows when you miss one

Every shake of the dressing bottle
sniff of the vegetable before we transform
its volume and shape
eggplant trouvaille
sometimes Italian words don't click into place
like Italy's government

The stir of the polenta is a tango warm-up
our legs know the routine
the dance of the kitchen witch
the sway of the dishtowel on our shoulder
masked in all that is fiery and ready for fight

My aunt sits and relaxes with an energy
most women don't have walking
my mom waits on roasted peppers
her lengthened lean
over her kitchen island
Scorpio principessa
my other aunt caresses the tablecloth
with her arthritic hands as she speaks
"More fennel."

If you're not used to it, you'll panic in the presence
the volume of our Italian stomp becomes a full-on
overture

ELAINA BATTISTA-PARSONS

flying hands, swerving waists
piling on pears and figs in between unshelled almonds
stuff your fucking face or we will cry
Stay out of our kitchens until we say it's safe
light a candle
clear the misfortunes—mallocchio
salt over junipers,
Hail Mary over sky
black tourmaline for grounding
as our ancestors stretch over our kitchen space
Mangia

Reapply your lipstick, ladies

QVC

It's sort of a meditation to sit with a warm cup of first coffee between five and seven a.m. and watch QVC in a silent house. Solace compared to an energetic evening. Mornings are always so much softer in temperament. My fireplace greets me with its cold stone. The thin tree branch outside the window slaps the vinyl on our house. Night can be so ambiguous and expectation-oriented, whereas morning opens its mind and lends you a sharp pencil.

QVC is skilled in making their sales hours feel like a social event for those who don't actually want to be social. The set, the conversations, the visuals around the product, which I guess are just props. A woman on a couch with her tea mug, two green houseplants on either side, her cozy sweater, and the way her light pink nails touch the necklace she is "pushing."

My friend got me hooked on the channel years ago. I only order maybe two products a year, so it's mostly an effective background noise when I write. And with each year the set grows more effective. Greenery outside the window behind the product display. A fireplace ready for snowstorms. Art selections on the wall behind. They raise the bar constantly.

Go on, QVC people. Tell me about the history of that three-tone Trinity pendant and how it found its way into American culture. Tell me about how you made those textured empanadas with your grandma in Mexico decades ago. Show me your freshly manicured oval gel nails as you twirl them over the fake diamond bangle that I'd buy and never wear. Or that I'd buy as a gift when I need it, but then forget I ever bought it. Explain the facet cuts of fake diamonds to me like a scientist.

Gourmet Holiday
you're a reminder
the world isn't so bad.
Feed me ... in installments
you pull me in as I sip
my French Roast and snuggle with my pup
over my keyboard and my manuscript
fuel my morning with a friendly wake-up
QVC old friend

Needle

I pulled the thin white thread
through the thin silver needle
through the fabric in my hands
and sewed my hope shut by accident

Any leftover buoyancy in me ceased
trapped between two pieces of
cotton blend Christmas patterns—
vintage red pick-up truck
in the snow and
gifts toppling over and under
stacked in festivity
trying to hide my
disappointment
and
lost hope for this global pandemic to
end

Duchess

I am the duchess of
snowfall
speaking secrets of the
icicle bible
covered in
winter sherbet and
pine needle crumbs

Sinking into a page of a novel about
lime seeds and witchery in the 1880s
the story feels true
like the snow outside
nothing realer than winter
in my soul

Finding the One

Year after year she seeks her match
but one is too bold
the other too meek

Strict
lazy
close-eared
"They always screw it up. Always," she says.

All so consistently inconsistent
planted in mediocre.

Year after year she swings
and misses
pendulum swing: *try this on,*
that one

or maybe this one

"This is it! I found her!"
but wait …
nope
too
cryptic
too ambitious
too serious
lemon balm, coconut mousse, vanilla glazed

"It's just your hair, Mom," I remind her.
"My hair is not easy to cut," she insists.

ELAINA BATTISTA-PARSONS

Quattro

Come Una Pregheira

Like a Prayer

Mom Guilt is Ugly

Moms need space too. Kids need *us* to need that space, I'm convinced of that after not having much space from them in 2020. They gather a sense of self from *our* sense of self because if not, they think we live for them alone. I *do* live for my children and my husband. To an extent. I also live for me. Without guilt. With volume. I still have dreams.

Stop the guilt over taking yourself for a walk or the guilt over taking a few hours on a Sunday to meet a friend for coffee and chatter. Stop the guilt over leaving for an entire Saturday to stroll or eat or do something alone or with a friend. Your family *will* survive and you'll return refueled.

"But not everyone needs that." Stop that. We're human beings and though we are driven to love and be together, we are also made up of a complex spirit that craves balance, whether we admit it or not. All of us have an individual spirit that requires maintenance.

My mom always made it known that she was a person of her own, and with that I realized I was my own person too, very early on. I refuse to do my daughter's laundry and make her weekly meals after she's eighteen. Doing their chores is not love. It's never letting them fully be who they are wholly meant to be. I mean let's say they're visiting from college for a weekend; of course, I'll throw their stuff in with a load of clothes, but beyond that. No. Hungry for lunch? Bread's on the counter, mozzarella's in the fridge.

Stop feeling guilty about being a person with needs
your needs show them
their needs so that everyone has their own space
Spirit,
Soul

STOP living for your kids every
second of your life
they don't want you to design every memory
they want a human being who highlights her eye shape
washes her hair, and
says—I need two hours of silence
to read. breathe. sleep. sip. watch. think.

"But you don't understand, I enjoy my kids."
umm so do I
stop making excuses
"But my kid is demanding."
then reteach them
give them more tools

That self-disrespect is going to make you
old
joyless
lonely
a wake up that
you forgot about YOU
no one's giving out awards
for most burnt-out mom
it's not admirable

That whole "hot mess" thing is worn out
and a pile of nonsense
stop
I say it all with love
I really do … because I want moms, dads
to remember their
own dreams and wishes and goals
in this very short time on Earth.

Things My Husband Says

It is amazing the contortions people will go through to admit there's a problem.

It is amazing the washing-over people will do to make themselves feel better.

It is amazing the way people ignore science and make their own information true.

Things I Say

Yet most amazing is how we still wake up and see the cardinal waiting for our cheek to twitch at its bright, miraculous head-tilt. Then we fail to emulate her. (I don't say those words out loud, don't worry.)

Husband:

Sometimes I need another male in the house

You guys feel an awful lot about everything. Feelings all the time.

Me:

But you're awesome with girls

You're meant for us. (I do say this out loud)

Husband:

And I love you all very much
But sometimes a guy needs a guy

To temper the constant feeling of feelings ... about feelings.

Wrapped in feelings.

Me:

You have the dog

ELAINA BATTISTA-PARSONS

Husband:

No, you have the dog.

(Dog is pasted to my side, it's true)

I love you.

Me:

U

Ery/Ary

Beanery, Apothecary, Patisserie, Winery
words that
give us
Sunday
and a fear of missing out
like,
a going-on
that if I'm not there, I fail
Farm to Table
Barn to Table
Fact and Fable

I haven't quite Thanksgiving-ed. Christmas-ed
Passover-ed
fun-dayed
weekend-ed

the way everyone else has
with their souvenir paper bag tied with baker's ribbon
"I've been out and about" look

A candle molded and flavored
in the likeness of their personal space—
In the Mood for Shove
Tango in the Blight
Sharpness of Words
Roses and Rants

Topiary
Aviary
cakery
my favorite is missing: Cemetery
so silent
free from all of this ARY/ERY noise

Pressure System

Meteorologists are poets in disguise
they couldn't find the words
so they found the masterpiece
in the heat waves and
pressure systems

Words and beats work
like moisture, current
air, wind
affecting people as heartily

Tides beating
like a verse riddled in knifepoint
storm
we are all in a storm

Candle Smoke

My house bristled in dead aunts
and nonnas who cast oregano spells
before me.

Teeming with old candle smoke
the sound of onions and oil

The equinox tastes like sage
but sounds like
my mom's garlic sizzling
before the tomato drop

Autumn speaks in flame
plum colored spirit
pencils between lines
exhalation from

Summer's pressured yellow burn

the dead ones like fall.
summer feels tired to them too

Dove Tree

Today I pulled the Dove Tree card:
blessings
but my morning exploded in Dread
cracked indigo
my face contorted like the brown candle bit
then in filtered the Peace—bubble by bubble
that blessing
promised by the Dove Tree card
tasted like mint and freedom
spitting the dread into
oblivion.

Sorelle

I only see it from a distance
a mess of arms
legs flailing
"Stoppppp"
love that's forever
encased in grass stains and
peach lip gloss
shared at the bus stop

Nights of gooey
white sugar sticks
over the fire pits

No one can puncture the
veil made of dandelions
gel pens and flashlights
glee made from a star
called Sister

Losing My Friend

I tried every single season to get him on a train, destination Jersey Shore from his apartment in Yardley.

The plan was I'd pick him up from the train tracks, and we'd drive my car to my house while we'd listen to his band's songs. His songs because his music is something to hear. It's Weezer meets Beck meets Beatles. It would ease his panic about being out in the world. We'd laugh, he'd express a little anxiety, but I'd comfort him. "You'll love my family." And he'd agree, then roll down the window for a smoke while I yelled at him that he'd get lung cancer if he didn't quit soon.

We'd get to my house and have a whiskey and pizza over the firepit in my yard.

He'd talk about the Beatles with my husband and smile with my girls. I'd drive him back to the train in the dark. All would feel rich. Cohesive.

But he never did get on those trains that I picked. Times. Dates. He never picked himself up from himself. Instead, we friend-shipped over text. We talked about ideas and art. Then I found out he died one night in January. And a chunk of my art-filled blood spilled out by the gallon. I still think of him every day. He's in my trees, my novels, and my above-air high panic when I cry in the dark. I know he hears me.

Ultimo

There's nothing I want more than love
There's nothing I want more than to be read and to read
There's nothing I want more
than my daughters to care and spread love
to speak up
to listen
to use people's pronouns with love
to treat everyone with respect
to be who they were meant to be

There's nothing I want more than to feel
I can die knowing
my girls know how to care when it counts
but also how to punch
hard when it counts
because they might need to in defense

I want them to know how to be themselves
in the most compassionate form possible
in the most thunderous way possible

Noon Bread

Growing up in a food-rich home has value. Even if it costs the grower-upper a few more pounds in the end. A few more pounds for when you strike a fever and can't eat for days. A few more pounds for the husband who likes a little cushion for the pushin'.

For gals with the noon bread in their lives, stop beating yourself up. You're feeding yourself, which is not a bad thing. My mother taught my brother and me what that means. To eat in and for joy. She taught us how to shove those leafy greens into our day. Her beautiful hard-working hands on the wheel in the kitchen without a cookbook or a plan. The ingredients were part of her instinct and memory of what she saw growing up. And she's passed it on. As I hope to do the same. Though baking is another creature. Not our jam.

I learned from my mom the beauty of a strawberry, what it means to hold it to the sunshine, over the colander, a view of the backyard's green majesty. The way a peach, perfectly ripe, can change your entire day, into the evening. You don't plate it. You slice it then eat it.

I learned from my mom how important our thumbs are to the constant peeling of mangoes and plums. I learned about the symbiosis among fruit and blood and vitality. I learned from my mom how to make food—medicine.

In our home, heavy cheese layers and red sauce wasn't the ticket. On special occasions my mom would make a lasagna, but I cannot remember a single baked ziti or frequent parmigiana dishes. Our brand of Italian was based in olive oil, lemons, onions, and garlic. Pasta with those items coated and delicious. We didn't eat heavily. I mean, sure she made her Sunday gravy/sauce. I don't care about that word choice. Other than that, she wasn't a "thick" cook. So many greens. So much olive oil. So many lemons and mushrooms and broccoli.

I'll never be thin
as long as bread and mozzarella Saturdays
exist in my land

ELAINA BATTISTA-PARSONS

of Italian-summer-world lunches
where curly-haired people with my DNA eat olives and
raw fennel by the pound before lunch is served
the bread disaster happens no matter how strong
the will—
post-beach in my parents' home
with old Julio Iglesias swimming in Portuguese ballads
cucumbers climbing over parsley
clean and folk-magical energy leaking across my
mom's original dinnerware
clean, excepting the ciabatta that threatens my
abdomen's fittest hours
erasing my jogs, so diligent and precise

to makes things worse,
the ciabatta is crisp and warm making cozy—
which inspires more bread
which stuffs the belly
which erases the beach morning that sparkled in
flat and clean, bikinied, blinded by sunshine over a
perfectly cool ocean
and my Tuscan cheeks shiny like olive oil in its
grandest aria
Italian and tan and muscular, even my torso

Bread—
for the ruins of
my thin dawn/my thin eight a.m./my thin ten a.m./
my empty 11:30 a.m., but for coffee
crushed dreams of a thin evening
battered and torn up by bread at noon

ELAINA BATTISTA-PARSONS

A note on My Italian Bones

I was in Italy for the first time in 1997.

Then again in 2000. My cousins gave me paradise.
The beach. The city. The food.

Someday I will see you again. Baci. Xoxo

Pierpaolo, Alessandra, Paola, Antonio, Andrea, and
in our hearts forever,

Leonardo.

Acknowledgements

Grazie. Thank you to everyone who showed up for me. First, to my husband and daughters. Kevin, without you … I don't know if this all would be possible. You give me the gift of time to do what I love. To my girls—love hard and fight for what you believe in. I love you all so very much.

Thank you to my mom, dad, and J.P. for the memories and the material. Thank you for the food, fabrics, and music.

Thank you, Benita Perez. Thanks for giving me the safe space to shout when I felt like it, and for letting me ask *why, how*, and *when*. Thank you Catie Daly, for your constant support and encouragement. Thank you to my friends who made me feel like I could keep going with this—Colleen, Chris, Danielle

B., Danielle G., Jean Gallos, Corinne, Jen S., Kim, Danica, Aris, Shea, Melissa R., Lillian, Liz, and Rev Lounge. Thank you to the TOFT community—I see you out there. Thank you, my amazing student Jack for cheering me on! Thank you KDM, Kate Ecke, and Aunt Grace for the strength you show and live as female leaders. Thank you Maria Taylor, Hank Parsons, Aunt Rose, and Cookie for your ongoing encouragement. Thank you Adena and Danita for the early *you can do its*. Thank you to my therapist, Sherri Goldman.

Thank you, Dakota Rayne, for getting this writing train on the tracks. You are the Goth Laverne to Melanie's Sunshine Shirley. Together, you'd rule the editing world.

Melanie Faith, my editor—you are more than any writer could ask for. You're brilliant, compassionate, and so very talented. Thank you to Jessica Bell and all of Vine Leaves Press for your belief in this project and for giving me my debut.

ELAINA BATTISTA-PARSONS

Vine Leaves Press

Enjoyed this book?

Go to *vineleavespress.com* to find more.